ERNST LUDWIG KIRCHNER — **A Retrospective Exhibition**

ERNST LUDWIG  KIRCHNER

a retrospective exhibition

by Donald E. Gordon

Seattle Art Museum
November 23, 1968–January 5, 1969

Pasadena Art Museum
January 16–February 23, 1969

Museum of Fine Arts, Boston
March 20–April 27, 1969

Contents

Preface

Our three museums have collaborated to present for the first time in widely diverse centers of the country a large number of Ernst Ludwig Kirchner's works in all media, spanning the course of his immensely productive career. In the light of our present understanding of modern art, it is hoped that his vast contributions to the art of Germany and to the culture of our century will be clearly unfolded.

The modern art of Germany has become increasingly well known in our time. The pioneering exhibition organized by Alfred H. Barr, Jr., at the Museum of Modern Art in 1931, only two years after its founding, formed an awareness of German achievements that has flourished in the post war years. Their monumental survey of twentieth century German art in 1957, organized by Andrew Carnduff Ritchie, brought to a new and more receptive generation greater definition and understanding. Meanwhile individual artists had already begun to receive attention and exposure. The outstanding Max Beckmann retrospective exhibition in St. Louis in 1948 (and subsequently shown in Los Angeles, Detroit, Minneapolis, and Baltimore), was followed by another in New York and Chicago in 1964. Similarly, studies in depth of the work of Nolde, Kokoschka, Kandinsky, Klee, Feininger and many others have been received enthusiastically by countless thousands of Americans over the past decade.

German expressionism, because of its radical departure from the entrenched naturalist tradition at the turn of the century and its persistent dominance of the visual arts in Germany, is a movement essential to an understanding of modern art. The expressionists, first the Brücke (Bridge) group born in Dresden in 1905 and the Blaue Reiter (Blue Rider) group formed in Munich in 1911, have captured the attention of the American audience.

As the focal figure of the Brücke Künstler-Gruppe, Kirchner stands in the pivotal position in that development. His passion to revitalize German art, his pursuit of humanistic truths instead of appearance, sought for new means of expression. His radical simplifications of space and form, absorption of primitivism and the power of symbolic color achieved a boldly personal vehicle. Kirchner's impact upon his contemporaries and succeeding movements has vitally affected the art of an entire generation.

While an abundance of Kirchner exhibitions in Europe reaches back fifty years, the first in America was launched at the Detroit Institute of Arts in 1937. That same year, Curt Valentin, newly emigrated from Germany, presented the first of his series of one-man exhibitions. He and, afterwards, Otto Gerson were of singular importance in establishing a magnificent tradition of support of Kirchner's art that extends even to the present. Thirteen years later Charles L. Kuhn organized a Kirchner exhibition at the Busch-Reisinger Museum of Harvard University, and in 1958, Wilhelm R. Valentiner, formerly Director of the Detroit Institute of Arts, presented a major retrospective exhibition at the North Carolina Museum of Art in Raleigh.

In size, broad span of representation, and appropriate emphasis on important periods, our exhibition is intended to clarify the goals, achievements and forces within the life and work of this master of our time.

Our three museums offer a profound debt of gratitude to the many individuals and institutions who have so generously sacrificed their own enjoyment to lend their works and support to our effort. Our gratitude will be joined by that of those thousands of Americans who will see the exhibition. We are also indebted to the German government for its sponsorship of the exhibition and financial support of part of its cost. We especially offer our thanks to its Ministers and Foreign Service officers for their most helpful efforts on our behalf. Our appreciation goes in particular to Dr. Donald E. Gordon, who has written the essay for the catalogue and who has given most generously of his knowledge and his energies toward the assembling of the exhibition and the documentation of the catalogue. No one has been more central to the accomplishment of the entire task than Thomas N. Maytham, Associate Director of the Seattle Art Museum. He has handled the arduous assignment of most of the correspondence; with undiminished zeal he pursued the reluctant lender and in the face of disappointment maintained a selection of works that has produced an exhibition admirable in balance and emphasis.

RICHARD E. FULLER,
President and Director
Seattle Art Museum

JAMES T. DEMETRION,
Director
Pasadena Art Museum

PERRY T. RATHBONE,
Director
Museum of Fine Arts, Boston

Lenders

Mr. and Mrs. Stephen Adler,
Holliswood, New York

Frau Hanna Bekker vom Rath,
Hofheim am Taunus, Germany

Mr. and Mrs. D. Thomas Bergen,
London

Mrs. William A. Bernoudy,
St. Louis

Mrs. Brigitta Valentiner Bertoia,
Barto, Pennsylvania

Ernesto Blohm,
Caracas

Dr. Carlo Bosshart,
Riehen, Switzerland

Lothar Günther Buchheim,
Feldafing, Germany

Wolfgang Budczies,
Bremen

Mr. and Mrs. John Cowles,
Minneapolis

Frau Edith Eucken-Erdsiek,
Freiburg

Dr. and Mrs. Ernst Fischer,
Albany

Mrs. Mariana Frenk-Westheim,
Mexico City

Karlheinz Gabler,
Frankfurt am Main

Dr. Rüdiger Graf von der Goltz,
Düsseldorf

Mr. and Mrs. Ernest Gottlieb,
New York

Kurt H. Grunebaum,
Harrison, New York

Walter Haller,
Biberach/Riss, Germany

Rätus Kern,
Zürich, Switzerland

Dr. Ulrich Kirchner,
Biberach/Riss, Germany

E. W. Kornfeld,
Bern

Mr. and Mrs. S. J. Levin,
St. Louis

Mr. and Mrs. Hall James Peterson,
Minneapolis

Mr. and Mrs. Perry T. Rathbone,
Cambridge, Massachusetts

David Rockefeller,
New York

Mrs. Heinz Schultz,
Great Neck, New York

Professor Hans Staub,
Zürich

Dr. Max M. Stern,
New York

Mrs. Ala Story,
Santa Barbara

Baron Heinrich Thyssen Bornemisza,
Lugano-Castagnola, Switzerland

Dr. Arthur Weisz,
New York

Anonymous Lenders

Achenbach Foundation for Graphic Arts,
California Palace of the Legion of Honor,
San Francisco

Albright-Knox Art Gallery,
Buffalo

Allen Memorial Art Museum, Oberlin College,
Oberlin, Ohio

Bayerische Staatsgemäldesammlungen,
Munich

Busch-Reisinger Museum, Harvard University

The Art Institute of Chicago

The Cleveland Museum of Art

The Detroit Institute of Arts

Fine Arts Museum, George Peabody College,
Nashville, Tennessee

Fogg Art Museum, Harvard University

Grunwald Graphic Arts Foundation,
University of California,
Los Angeles

Hamburger Kunsthalle

Hessisches Landesmuseum,
Darmstadt

Von der Heydt Museum der Stadt Wuppertal

Kunstsammlung Nordrhein-Westfalen,
Düsseldorf

Landschaft Davos,
Switzerland (Municipality of Davos)

Marion Koogler McNay Art Institute,
San Antonio

Milwaukee Art Center

The Minneapolis Institute of Arts

Museum of Art, Carnegie Institute,
Pittsburgh

Museum of Fine Arts,
Boston

The Museum of Modern Art,
New York

North Carolina Museum of Art,
Raleigh

Oeffentliche Kunstsammlung,
Basel

Pasadena Art Museum

Pfalzgalerie,
Kaiserslautern

Scottish National Gallery of Modern Art,
Edinburgh

Seattle Art Museum

Smith College Museum of Art,
Northampton, Massachusetts

Staatliche Kunsthalle,
Karlsruhe

Staatsgalerie,
Stuttgart

Städtische Galerie,
Frankfurt am Main

Wallraf-Richartz-Museum,
Cologne

Galerie Wolfgang Ketterer,
Munich

Felix Landau Gallery,
Los Angeles

Marlborough-Gerson Gallery Inc.,
New York

Galerie Nierendorf,
Berlin

Galerie Springer,
Berlin

Foreword

The Ernst Ludwig Kirchner retrospective exhibition has been organized on the occasion of the thirtieth anniversary of the artist's death in 1938, to provide a fresh and extensive examination of one of the most revolutionary and influential figures in the development of German expressionist art. As leader of Die Brücke, Kirchner's work has been seen, although infrequently, by American audiences since the 1930's, while in Europe a multitude of exhibitions, many of vast dimensions, have been organized. Only now, more than sixty years after the Brücke movement was founded and three decades after Kirchner's death, is an exhibition of appropriately large scale and broad representation presented to the American public. It is in addition the first exhibition to be seen at points spanning the length and breadth of the land. While quality alone has been the uppermost criterion in all media, we have sought to include outstanding available works in European collections, most of which have never been publicly exhibited in America. We have attempted as well to represent the many media in which Kirchner worked: oil, watercolor, gouache, pastel, drawings in crayon, ink, and pencil; of his vast production of prints, forty woodcuts, etchings, and lithographs; and two sculptures in wood.

The exhibition was conceived several years ago by James T. Demetrion, then Curator of the Pasadena Art Museum, who actively pursued the project with Dr. Donald E. Gordon of Dickinson College. Organization of the exhibition was placed in the hands of Gerald Nordland, Director of the Washington (D.C.) Gallery of Modern Art, and then his successor, Charles Millard. Interruption of their exhibition schedule ultimately provided the opportunity for me to organize it in Seattle. Throughout, the concept of the exhibition has been sustained by Dr. Gordon, whose

scholarship and interest in Kirchner's art has formed the cornerstone of our collaborative effort. He has written the essay for the catalogue, has selected the paintings and often offered valuable advice regarding works in the other media, and has served invaluably in obtaining loans from Europe. The exhibition coincides with his publication of a critical study and the first catalogue raisonné of Kirchner's oil paintings (Harvard University Press and Prestel-Verlag, Munich). Individual entries on the oil paintings in our catalogue are based on those in his book, and the dates given to works in the exhibition are his. In like manner, our bibliography is selected from the book's comprehensive list. We are of course indebted to Harvard University Press for permission to use this material, and to Gustav Stresow, Director of Prestel-Verlag, for the loan of several color plates and for numerous kindnesses to Dr. Gordon on behalf of the exhibition.

Because of the long acknowledged practice of the artist in his later years to ascribe inaccurately early dates to many of his works, the question of the correct chronology of his *œuvre* has remained problematic. Dr. Gordon's book, our exhibition and its catalogue incorporate a decade of European and American research in this area, since the Valentiner exhibition at Raleigh in 1958, in order to sort out these problems through concerted stylistic analysis and documentary support.

Our primary debt of gratitude is to the many lenders, private and public, too numerous to thank here individually, who have made their separate sacrifices of works in their collections on behalf of the American public, and in added tribute to the memory of Kirchner and his genius. An exhibition of this duration has demanded special generosity on their part. Among the lenders, Dr. Gordon and I wish to extend our deep appreciation to the heirs of the artist for their singular kindness in granting the loan of rarely seen paintings. I wish to offer my gratitude as well to Wolfgang Budczies, Dr. Ernst Fischer, Dr. Rüdiger Graf von der Goltz, Florian Karsch, and William Lieberman and Dorothy Miller of the Museum of Modern Art, New York, for their especially generous loans. To the government of the German Federal Republic special appreciation is owed for its sponsorship of the exhibition and partial subsidy of its costs. In that regard, our thanks go to Dr. Karl Gustav Gerold, formerly of the German Foreign Office in Bonn, to Dr. Hasso Freiherr von Maltzahn of that Office and to Dr. Hans-Joachim Falk, First Secretary of the German Embassy, Washington, D.C.

To the Directors of the three participating museums, I offer my thanks for their support in the organization of the exhibition: to Dr. Richard E. Fuller for his ready permission for me to organize and present it in Seattle; to James Demetrion for his suggestions and willing assistance in obtaining loans; and especially to Perry T. Rathbone, long an advocate of German expressionist art, for numerous loans from his museum and personal collection, for assistance in obtaining additional loans and for generously committing his staff to many of the myriad problems involved with an exhibition of this dimension. My thanks go to his assistants Miss Virginia Fay and Mrs. Tamsin McVicker, to Miss Mary O'Neill, Registrar at the Boston Museum, to Charles E. Humphrey, Comptroller, and especially to Carl F. Zahn for his design of the catalogue, and to Mrs. Angelica Rudenstine, former Editor of Publications and her assistant Mrs. Marian Martin.

In the course of preparation, numerous persons have contributed significantly in various ways to the success of the exhibition. I wish to express my appreciation to the late René d'Harnoncourt and to William Rubin for their support, to Anthony Clark of the Minneapolis Institute of Arts and to Samuel Sachs and Edward Foster of his staff, to Dr. Werner Haftmann, James B. Byrnes and Leonard Hutton for their assistance or advice. In Seattle, Mrs. Sue Kent has been especially valuable in the preparation of the catalogue, and Miss Antoinette Alexander has helped effectively in all stages of the project.

Thomas N. Maytham,
Director of the Exhibition
Seattle Art Museum

Introduction
and
Chronology

The Dresden Period

A fundamental guideline in the development of modern styles by European painters after 1900 was a formal one: the concept of a picture as being, before anything else, "a flat surface covered with colors arranged in a certain order."[1] This affirmation of the decorative principle in painting was strangely alien to German artists at the outset of the twentieth century—involved as they were either with the content of their art, or with more or less naturalistic styles in which vestiges of three-dimensional illusion were essential. Henri Matisse at Collioure in 1905, Pablo Picasso and Georges Braque in Paris and l'Estaque in 1907–8, and Wassily Kandinsky at Murnau around 1909 first consistently asserted the absolute primacy of the picture plane, building on strong decorative and abstract traditions from the late nineteenth century, and affirming pictorial laws which were to affect the art of their entire generation. But none was German in nationality and outlook. Under the circumstances, then, particular stress must be placed on the accomplishment of a two-dimensionalized style by Kirchner in Dresden. Between about 1905 and 1909 in Germany it was Kirchner who first and most consistently insisted upon the decorative logic of the painting surface; following his leadership, the Brücke helped reinforce this quality in the work of a new German modern art.

It was through work in drawing, particularly in rapid sketches from life, that Kirchner first developed appropriate linear and planar abbreviations for forms in nature. These abbreviations, which he called hieroglyphs, were evolved gradually during the Brücke years. Some could be utilized readily in one or the other of the graphic media, others were appropriately incorporated into his painting vocabulary, but their origin is almost always to be found in the drawing sketchbooks which he usually had at hand. Kirchner drew as other men write. His artistic styles in all media could change in accordance with changes in his linear handwriting, and these changes could have many different causes, due either to ephemeral or deepseated stimuli, to external influence or wholly personal mood or feeling. Granted this capacity for variation in linear attack, Kirchner approached color in a similar manner: seemingly spontaneous, his color choice and composition always reveal the painter as much as his sources.

Through an increasingly two-dimensionalized and hieroglyphic formal vocabulary, in turn, Kirchner gained an unexpected freedom to explore the expressive aspects of art. Like their contemporaries in Paris and Munich, the Brücke artists built upon certain subjectivist traditions innovated by post-impressionist painters during the 1880's and 1890's. But where "decoration" and "expression" were essentially synonymous for Matisse and other French fauve artists, (in the sense intended by Paul Cézanne), Kirchner and his Dresden friends came ultimately to value self-expression in the creative process more highly and for its own sake—seeing the work of art as bridge between self and world (in the *synthétiste* sense of Paul Gauguin). Among the Brücke artists, especially Kirchner insisted on the simultaneous heightening of both the decorative and the expressive aspects of each art work. His answers to this challenge formed his Brücke style.

[1] Maurice Denis, *Theories, 1890–1910*, Paris, 1912, p. [3].

A Brücke Painting

Among Kirchner's first life-size multifigure compositions in painting was the *Street, Dresden* (Cat. no. 12), most probably created late in the year 1908. It is contemporary with the painting *Dodo and Her Brother* (Cat. no. 11), in the Smith College Museum. The *Dodo* itself is interesting in its own right, both for the masklike male face in intense green with red outlining (not unknown in Van Dongen's and Munch's earlier work), and for its figure types. The male figure's stance—widely separated legs against horizontal floor plane with one leg and foot sharply foreshortened—derives directly from a Munch male portrait exhibited in the 1908 Berliner Sezession. The representation of Dodo unexpectedly combines a frontal head and body with a near profile view of lower torso— emphasized by allowing the profile leg contours to show through her dress: this figure convention can derive only from ancient Egyptian or other near eastern precedent.

Kirchner had these specific elements in mind when he set about composing the Museum of Modern Art *Street, Dresden*. The major female figure in dark green dress, placed just to the right of the centerline of the composition, is essentially a mirror image of the female figure in the Smith College painting: Dodo's fan now becomes a purse and the other arm is hidden, but the same three-quarter view of the lower torso is presented with the bulge of the thigh now on the left. Similarly, the adjacent woman in enormous hat and light jacket becomes the counterpart to the male figure in the Northampton painting: the petticoats revealed by the raised skirt echo the shape between his widely spaced legs, while the unearthly green face outlined and accented in red is taken over directly from the face of Dodo's brother. The spatial construction of the *Street* is

also derived in part from this source. The horizontal accents behind the lower torsos in the double portrait are recapitulated in the group scene by a line marking the lower skirt edge of the small female figure upper right, and carried across to the two feet of the child in the center; this line is approximated again at the left in the baseline of the female figure seen from the back. But the wall plane of the *Dodo,* marking the limits of spatial recession in that picture, now merely marks a friezelike middleground plane through which openings into more distant space are intentionally cut. One of the most beautifully composed of all Kirchner spatial conceptions, design on the surface and in depth are thus masterfully coordinated. The projection downward and forward of the two major figures just to the right of center is neatly balanced by the greatest penetration of space upward and into the picture just to the left of this line. Similarly, the negative shape of the ground-plane between and below the right-hand figures, with its curvilinear sweep slightly upward to the right, is transposed into the similar positive shapes of the two women pedestrians distinguished from the crowd on the left.

This integrated surface design is still further transformed into a richly orchestrated pattern of movement. Starting with the halted streetcar, top center, the staccato and isolated pedestrian movement in the distance is rendered backwards, sideways, and, in the small child center, forward to the left. Then, with strictly frontal movement stressed only for the small female figure in the upper right, the nearer woman in white moves toward the left; the central female figure is made to face slightly to the right; while the largest male figure is cut by the frame as he sweeps off the lower right-hand corner of the composition. The curvilinear rhythm within the design, set in motion by the large arcs of the women's varied hats

1909

January: first one-man exhibition outside France by Henri Matisse, held in the Cassirer Gallery, Berlin; Kirchner in Berlin briefly at this time. Brücke graphic art first included in the Berliner Sezession 1908–9 winter show. Heckel visits Italy. June: Brücke group exhibition in the Richter Salon, where Kirchner's leadership of the group towards a German fauve style is mentioned by a critic. Summer: Heckel, Kirchner, and their models live and work in the Moritzburg Lake district outside Dresden; two young orphan girls, Marcella and Fränzi, become Brücke models. Brücke studios in the Berliner Strasse, Dresden, are decorated with draperies and other ornament derived from primitive New Guinea and African sources seen in the Dresden Ethnographical Museum. Small scale sculptures, cast of tin, and carved wood studio furniture, both in 1909, soon followed by Kirchner's first wood sculptures.

1910

Increasing interest in primitive art sources. May: the first Neue Sezession exhibition, Berlin, including all the Dresden Brücke painters and Pechstein's Berlin followers, marks the emergence of the Brücke as the leading avant-garde group in the German capital; through this exhibition, Otto Mueller in Berlin becomes Kirchner's friend and a Brücke member; through Mueller, Kirchner attracted to the art of Lucas Cranach. Summer: second summer of communal work at the Moritzburg Lakes, including Kirchner, Pechstein, Heckel and, probably, Mueller. September: last Brücke group exhibition in Dresden, the first to be held in the Arnold Gallery. September: twenty-six paintings by Paul Gauguin, primarily from Tahiti, also exhibited in the Arnold Gallery. Kirchner explores additional non-western art (including Benin and Egyptian sources) to discover illustrations of Buddhist wall-paintings from the cave-temples of Ajanta, India.

1911

Woodcuts and a drawing by Kirchner illustrated in the avant-garde Berlin magazine, *Der Sturm*; continuing Brücke participation in the Berlin Neue Sezession and its exhibitions. Summer: Kirchner's first trip outside Germany, a brief visit to Bohemia (including Prague) with Mueller; last Brücke excursion to Moritzburg, probably limited to Kirchner and Heckel. Autumn: Kirchner moves permanently from Dresden to Berlin, as do Heckel and Schmidt-Rottluff; Pechstein and Kirchner form an unsuccessful art school. In Berlin Kirchner meets Erna Schilling, who becomes his Berlin model and lifetime companion.

12
Street (Strasse), ca. 1908
The Museum of Modern Art, New York.

11
Dodo and Her Brother (Dodo und ihr Bruder),
ca. 1908
Smith College Museum of Art, Northampton,
Massachusetts.

8
Man Resting, Portrait of Hans Frisch (Ruhender
Mann, Hans Frisch), ca. 1907
Marion Koogler McNay Art Institute, San Antonio.

comes to a focus, vortexlike, at the center of the composition. Here, between the little girl and the woman in green, the latter's shoulder is transformed into a convex shape, emphasized by a bright green outline and repeated in an adjacent black shape, to provide a springboard for the concentric ellipses of pink road and ornamented hat above the child's head. The surging curvilinear movement spiraling out from this vortex, and animating the contours of figures in all parts of the composition, provides that restless dynamism central to the picture's vitality.

A year later than the *Portrait of Hans Frisch* (Cat. no. 8), this movement of line and color ensnares the myriad human subjects. Not only the world of nature but its inhabitants as well have become alien. In spite of new and original compositional methods, in spite of the use of line and color ultimately synthetist and fauve (rather than symbolist), in spite of the fashionable clothes and the youthful canon of feminine beauty in the largest figure, the picture expresses the same *Angst* of modern man as its prototype, Munch's *Spring Evening on Karl-Johann Street.*

The porcine male figure seen in bloated profile in the upper right-hand corner of the Kirchner composition is a type which fascinated Picasso in his monumental painting of 1905 entitled *Les Saltimbanques.* Had Picasso chosen to follow a more personal line of expression in 1908, rather than repressing it in the interest of cubist intellectualization, he might well have come even closer in expression (though not in content) to Kirchner's *Street.* For it is uncanny how many parallels there are between *Les Saltimbanques* (which Kirchner could hardly have known) and the German painting under discussion. Reading from left to right in the French work, one sees an extended hand, a figure viewed from the back with lowered right arm, the aforementioned older male figure, a single frontal youth surrounded by void, and a female figure with strangely inappropriate hat resting lightly on her hair. These are all elements used, in other positions, by Kirchner. In spite of their differences of style and of expression, the two independent works show how universal the sense of the alienation of modern man from his kind and from his environment at this time actually was. And yet, in contrast to Picasso's classic, courtly approach towards woman, Kirchner allows woman the daemonic to dominate. Woman as child-virgin, woman as nubile aggressive symbol, and woman as crone here comprise Kirchner's dominant trio. Unconsciously reflecting Munch's *Three Ages of Woman,* Kirchner gives us in the *Street* a timeless myth clothed in modern dress. Like all Brücke paintings, this is thus more than a depiction of contemporary Dresden city life. Informed by decorative logic and expressive vitality, it is a picture which speaks in what Kirchner called the universal language of symbolic form. It is also a masterpiece of modern art, with which the artist could not part during his lifetime.

The Expressionist Period

If Kirchner's first period before late 1911 was largely international in outlook, the work of the next dozen years (half in Berlin, half in Switzerland) may be characterized as the artist's mature contribution to a national German culture in the twentieth century. That culture is no easier to label than it is to define. In painting it has been called *Ausdruckskunst*, "an art of emotional expression," or else expressionism (originally meaning "an art of self-expression") —and the confusion has been compounded by the expansion of the latter term to include both meanings. At the same time, overall German culture of the period between 1910–11 and 1923 has too often been considered monolithic, ignoring distinctions between realist and neoromantic origins and tendencies, between art of the ivory tower and art of political activism, and between the different media of artistic expression. Kirchner came to expressionism from the realist rather than the romantic direction; even at the height of his personal suffering in 1916 he still wished to create an ordered picture of his times. His art was quintessentially personal and apolitical, devoid of socialist or, later, Nazi sympathies, although often informed with an understanding of the sufferings of persecuted individuals of all races and nationalities. And his contribution—unlike that of, say, Ernst Barlach or Oskar Kokoschka—was made in the visual arts alone. Beginning gradually in Berlin, but with its roots in earlier Dresden experience, Kirchner's art sprang from an increasing awareness of what may be called "existential man"—no longer the "psychological man" of the previous realist generation.[2] Paralleling the development in German philosophy from Edmund Husserl's phenomenology (between 1901 and 1913) to the existentialist positions of Martin Buber (between 1909 and 1923) and of Husserl's student Martin Heidegger (in 1927), Kirchner's expressionist art operates most directly on the level of intense personal experience.

In many Berlin and early Swiss portraits Kirchner developed extraordinary pictorial methods with which to project his own existential awareness into his subjects or, through empathy, to attempt to express the inwardly experienced uniqueness of others. If "the aim of expressionism is to give voice to this indefinable 'inner feel,' this translogical essential situation,"[3] then Kirchner successfully achieved this expressionist goal more profoundly and more consistently than any other pictorial artist of his generation. It is this which best explains his continuing relevance in the second half of the twentieth century to a new generation which suffers the same existential crisis that the expressionists discovered in themselves more than half a century earlier.

Perhaps the closest analogue to Kirchner's Berlin and Swiss expressionist paintings are the "calmly controlled nightmares"[4] which Franz Kafka created in Prague and Berlin during these same dozen years. Like Kafka, Kirchner was one of the relatively few artists and writers of his generation whose artistic talent was sufficient to realize fully his artistic purpose; disciplined and effective form was the vehicle in the work of both artists, not the unbridled emotionalism or apocalyptical extremity of some others. Yet in the final analysis the existentially similar loneliness, withdrawal, and disguises of these near-contemporaries had different re-

[2] Paul Kornfeld, "Der beseelte und der psychologische Mensch," *Das junge Deutschland,* I, 1918, p. 1 ff.

[3] Walter H. Sokel, *The Writer in Extremis; Expressionism in Twentieth-Century German Literature,* Stanford, 1959, p. 54.

[4] *Ibid.,* p. 4.

1912

January: meeting with Franz Marc in Berlin. March: participation in the second *Blaue Reiter* exhibition, Galerie Hans Goltz, Munich, and in that group's famous almanac edited by Marc and Kandinsky. April: Brücke group exhibition, Galerie Fritz Gurlitt, Berlin (later shown at the Galerie Commeter, Hamburg); Kirchner and Heckel execute the chapel mural-paintings for the Sonderbund International Art Exhibition in Cologne. May: Kirchner meets Munch at the opening of the Sonderbund exhibition, which presented modern art from fourteen countries under the label of expressionism. Summer: extended visit to Fehmarn with Erna, where a more sensuous and sculpturesque style, fusing Ajanta and African prototypes, comes to fruition. Autumn: exploration of Cézannesque and cubist formal principles, before developing methods of radical spatial distortion; increasing contact with leading expressionist writers, including Alfred Döblin. Neue Sezession dissolved.

1913

February: one painting represented in the American Armory Show in New York (later traveling to Chicago and Boston). May: the Brücke group formally disbanded. Summer: Kirchner and Erna again at Fehmarn. Autumn: possibly stimulated by Italian futurist works exhibited in Berlin, Kirchner begins a series of major Berlin street scenes which extend into 1914; his first one-man exhibitions are held in the Folkwang Museum, Hagen, and Galerie Gurlitt, Berlin.

sults, transcending the basic difference in their chosen media of expression. Apparently no one acquainted with the efficient clerk Kafka in his anonymous office routine suspected the creative despair of the author privately too unsure of his greatness to publish. No one exposed to the morbid mistrust of Kirchner in Berlin, Kreuzlingen, or the "Lärchen" house knew that he thought of his art as a way of declaring his love for humanity. While Kafka's fear was that excessive introspection might lead to madness, for Kirchner the danger was that excessive feeling might lead to self-destruction. Maturity brought existential nightmares to both artists, but Kirchner experienced them with less outward calm during the war years than did Kafka, and he awoke from them eventually afterward, as Kafka did not.

Though completely committed to self-expression, Kirchner would never completely reject either the world of nature or the possibility that his art might communicate from self to other. His formal vocabulary was to retain a kind of pictorial logic throughout the 1911–23 period which remained as accessible to cerebral as to emotional comprehension. More like Matisse and Paul Klee than like Nolde or Wassily Kandinsky, he was a leader of his artistic generation while only rarely being an extremist.

A Berlin Painting

Berlin on the eve of world war was a vortex of change, both destructive and creative: "the prophetic Cassandra-like mood of [pictorial] artists makes their work a document of artistic premonition. They seem to us now to have been dancing on a volcano whose eruptions were anticipated in violent rhythms and inner excitement. Burdened

with such a fateful mission, their art excites rather than gives comfort."[5] New naval armament and political realignment among the great powers made the possibility of military warfare a subject for increasing European speculation: primarily German artists first felt this premonition as threat rather than as adventure or necessity. Kirchner's Berlin street scenes from late 1913, for which he is today most famous, must be understood against this background.

The first three paintings in this series were most probably those now in Cologne (Wallraf-Richartz-Museum; not exhibited) in Frankfurt (Cat. no. 40), and *Street, Berlin* in the Museum of Modern Art, New York (Cat. no. 41). Four of the five fashionably dressed women in the Cologne picture are placed in a spatial rhombus, two of whose sides meet in an apex on the sidewalk below, while the fifth figure stands to the right peering into a store window. The spatial rhombus, but not the right-hand figure, is retained in the Frankfurt composition. Especially the Cologne work stresses the isolation of the prominently vertical figures on the picture plane and in space, but angular distortions in both paintings create nervously animated pictorial rhythms. In the New York version of the theme, the right-hand figure (now male) is reinstated, and accessory background figures from the Frankfurt picture are multiplied. But the spatial rhombus is eliminated so that, for the first time in the series, three-dimensional tensions are subordinated to two-dimensional ones.

Here is one key to *Street's* pictorial effectiveness. The two women and nearest man clearly establish a foreground plane, yet none of them comprises a major vertical accent; instead they are composed on the surface in two opposing

[5] Jakob Rosenberg, "German Expressionist Printmakers," *Magazine of Art*, XXXVIII/8, 1945, p. 302.

41
The Street (Die Strasse), ca. 1913
The Museum of Modern Art, New York.

diagonal complexes, meeting in an angle of a-
bout 40 degrees. The lines of the cab on the left
and, especially, of the male background figures,
are organized within this same system of sharply
angular coordinates. The complex design struc-
ture of "V," "A," "Z," "N," and "M" shapes is
completely reinforced by the angular stylizations
of noses, chins, and hats, and by the pointed
shapes of feet and hands. The zigzag qualities
of the brushstrokes (generally characteristic of
the early Berlin style as a whole) are thus here
utterly consistent with the two-dimensional shape
conception. The activity, force, and movement
inherent in the subject are made radically explosive by their compression towards the design
surface.

One of the hallmarks of Kirchner's Berlin style,
departing from the Dresden usage of primary
hues in supplementary or complementary combination, is his limitation of each painting to hues
adjacent on the color circle. In *Street, Berlin* the
full daemonic possibilities of adjacent color are
most forcefully realized. Aside from the graphic
dimension of pure white and black, the interplay
is between the rich dark blues of the central figures and the intense colors of the sidewalk;
though ranging from crimson to cerise, they are
dominated by an acrid scarlet. The purple robe
of the nearest figure (whose hair is red) is the
necessary median to these adjacent hues. The
color combination is thus caustic, raw, electric.
In spite of their conscious elegance in grooming
and costuming, these figures too are prisoners—
no longer prisoners of their stylistic isolation, as
in the Cologne work, but captives of the electric,
vitalist force of the street itself. Earlier, Kirchner
had found the deserted *Street in Schöneberg City
Park* (Cat. no.35) filled with the melancholy of
the big city; now the metropolitan street denies
all human emotion. Instead, like a gigantic dyna-
mo blindly pulsing current and unseen light, it
transforms its occupants into dehumanized mari-
onettes.

35
Street in Schöneberg City Park, Innsbruck Street
(Strasse am Stadtpark Schöneberg, Innsbrucker
Strasse), ca. 1912–13
Milwaukee Art Center (Gift of Mrs. Harry Lynde
Bradley).

1914

February: one-man exhibition at the Art Association, Jena, where he meets Eberhard Grisebach, Professor Botho Gräf, the poet Carl Theodore Bluth, and others instrumental in establishing his nationwide reputation. Spring: decorative commission at the Werkbund exhibition in Cologne. Summer: last Fehmarn visit with Erna, cut short by the outbreak of World War I. Named as a pioneer of German expressionism in Paul Fechter's book, *Der Expressionismus* (Munich: Piper Verlag, 1914). First acquaintance with Oskar Schlemmer.

1915

Military training as an artillery driver in Halle, ended by physical and nervous collapse. Back in his studio in October, evolves wartime expressionist style with expanded thematic range; creates color woodcut illustrations to Chamisso's "Peter Schlemihl." Brief visits to Dr. Kohnstamm's sanatorium in Königstein near Frankfurt am Main, and to Jena. Friendship with Carl Hagemann, who provides the artist with a monthly allowance for two years and who later assembles the largest Kirchner art collection in Germany.

1916

Peripatetic travels to Halle, Jena, and Königstein; at the Kohnstamm institution in July he completes a series of five frescoes based on Fehmarn subjects. Friendship with the expressionist novelist Carl Sternheim. October: Kirchner's first exhibition at the Galerie Ludwig Schames, Frankfurt (as Kirchner's dealer, Schames mounts eight exhibitions from 1916 to 1925); also in Frankfurt, Mrs. Rosi Fischer begins her major Kirchner collection. December: unable to respond to a second military conscription, Kirchner placed in a Berlin sanatorium.

1917

January: brief visit to Dr. Lucius Spengler in Davos, Switzerland, seeking medical care. February: struck by an automobile in Berlin, the artist experiences increasing lameness in arms and legs. May: return to Davos; friendship with Henry Van de Velde, who provides financial and moral support during the artist's early Swiss years. Summer: in a rented mountain farmhouse on the Staffelalp near Frauenkirch, just south of Davos, Kirchner able to execute only a few woodcuts. Autumn: from September on, a patient at Bellevue sanatorium in Kreuzlingen, Switzerland, under the care of Dr. Ludwig Binswanger; during a visit by Erna in October, Kirchner catalogues his earlier art works from memory (misdating many of them) and empowers her legally to conduct his Berlin affairs for him; his will is dated November 1st. His paralyzed limbs make impossible the completion of works other than woodcuts, yet some of the latter in ensuing months are among his masterpieces. Friendship at Kreuzlingen with Leonhard Frank and other expressionist writers. December: agreement by Gustav Schiefler, cataloguer of Munch's and Nolde's prints, to catalogue Kirchner's graphic work.

1918

March: first major exhibition in Switzerland, twenty-two works at the Zürich Kunsthaus. July: permitted to leave the Kreuzlingen sanatorium accompanied by an attendant, Kirchner returns to the Staffelalp mountain house, where many of the early Swiss paintings are conceived (though few are yet completed); first signs of improvement in his physical condition. October: move to the farmhouse *In den Lärchen* ("among the larch-trees") on the Längematte near Frauenkirch, where he lives for five years. Late expressionist style develops in alpine landscapes; woodcut series of illustrations to Petrarch's "Triumph of Love."

A Lärchen Painting

The Detroit Institute of Arts' *Winter Moon Landscape* (Cat. no. 49), like the color woodcut of the same subject (Cat. no. 134), is a square-format composition in sweeping rhythms of reds, blues, yellows, and silvery whites. The crystalline snow in the foreground and the distant mountain peaks, respectively rendered in whites and in blues modeled in violet, evoke that sense of limitless grandeur and awesome stillness so characteristic of the Alps in moonlight. But the subject, almost apocalyptical in mood, betrays the subjective quality of Kirchner's personal interpretation. The sky in intensely rich reds and browns and the staccato puffs of circular ocher and yellow clouds around the moon (supplemented by the eerie pinks and reds used for the large trees which march unbrokenly to the sky on the right) provide an important expressional dimension to the work. *Winter Moon Landscape* was conceived early on the morning of January 20, 1919, as we know from Kirchner's published letters.[6] Supposedly secure and remote in his Alpine retreat, he was yet emotionally involved with the turbulent events in Berlin which Erna communicated from their studio: joy at the European armistice amidst a bitter and deadly (if eventually abortive) socialist revolution. No matter how awe inspiring the moonlit landscape appeared to him early that morning, these letters (like so many others by the artist) reveal the peculiarly modern predicament of a sensitive man, in an environment no longer permitting geographic escape or full inner security. They allow us rare insight into the process by which a peaceful subject is empathically ani-

[6] E. L. Kirchner, *Briefe an Nele*, Munich, 1961, p. 14 ff.; Lothar Grisebach, ed., *Maler des Expressionismus in Briefwechsel mit Eberhard Grisebach*, Hamburg, 1962, p. 98.

49
Winter Moon Landscape (Wintermondnacht), 1919
The Detroit Institute of Arts (Gift of Curt Valentin on
the 60th Birthday of Dr. W. R. Valentiner).

27

mated with the daemonic overtones of a world in which people can dance admist machine-gun fire. An Alpine mountain is not conceived with romantic pantheism, as it would have been in the previous century, but as a neutral screen on which are projected the frightening shock-waves of a crazed continent.

1919–1920
Receives his hand-presses in January; Erna supervises the shipment of the contents of the Berlin studio to Kirchner in the Lärchen house, and joins him there in the course of 1919. He carves almost all the house furniture, unifying function and ornament in wood sculpture. Begins a regular diary and articulates his personal ideas on art, soon published under his own name or that of the pseudonymous L. de Marsalle. March 1920: painting of theater backdrops for local dramatic groups. The Dutch painter Jan Wiegers among the first artists to seek Kirchner's tutelage and friendship during the Swiss years.

1921–1923
His health fully restored, the artist is active in the cultural life of the Davos region and (at a distance) the German art world. The late expressionist style, tempered by increasing work from nature, develops in more decorative and monumental directions to culminate in 1923 in several thirteen-foot paintings, *Sunday in the Alps*. February 1921: fifty works exhibited at the Kronprinzenpalais, Berlin. Summer 1921: first Swiss work from the nude in a landscape setting. 1922: meeting and friendship with Dr. Frederic Bauer, Davos physician and Kirchner's major Swiss collector; woodcut illustrations to the expressionist books *Neben der Heerstrasse* (1923) by Kirchner's friend and neighbor Jakob Bosshart, and the posthumous edition of *Umbra Vitae* (1924) by Germany's foremost early expressionist poet, Georg Heym. June 1923: fifty works exhibited at the Kunsthalle in Basel (leading to frequent visits over the next three years by young Basel artists known as the Red-Blue group). Autumn 1923: Kirchner and Erna move to the Wildboden house in Frauenkirch valley.

The Wildboden Period

Western Europe entered a general period of cultural relaxation during the early 1920's. The characteristics of the next dozen years were projected in the first surrealist manifesto in Paris and the first "new objectivity" exhibition in Mannheim, both in 1924, and the publication, in 1922, of the first stream-of-consciousness novel—Joyce's *Ulysses*. Though progressive, these movements were noticeably less dynamic than the dada, futurist, and expressionist points of view which had flourished earlier. The revolutionary changes in all the arts just before the First World War required a full generation for elaboration and adjustment at a slower pace and with less frenzied experimentation. Thus, artists who came to full maturity during the postwar period (such as Klee, Miro, and T. S. Eliot) appear publically old beyond their years compared to such exuberantly optimistic figures as Boccioni, Marc, and Apollinaire who went before. Concomitantly the new age was primarily form oriented—concerned less now with what was said than with how it was stated or shaped. From the Bauhaus to atonal music in the arts and from Berenson to the Oxford critics in cultural exegesis, Europe was obsessed with the outward appearance and function of things and tended to circumscribe inner complexity and radical ideas. It was not that artists stopped feeling or lost interest in meaning; it was that they no longer tried to involve the public in this meaning or, if they tried, that they did not succeed in doing so. Form and function dominated the aesthetics of a conservative industrial society at peace; its cultural aristocracy was created on the basis of sensitivity to esoteric form, not metaphysical, humanistic, or spiritual meaning. In this deceivingly stable age form and content were unnaturally divided, with content relegated to a lower order: many germinal ideas maturing belatedly in this milieu—such as Heidegger's existentialism, Jung's archetypal symbol, and Panofsky's iconological interpretation —had to await the chaos of Spain, Poland, and Pearl Harbor before capturing the minds of a new generation in the period to come. F. L. Wright, D. H. Lawrence, and J. P. Sartre were out of place in the age of Virginia Woolf, Mondrian, and the concept of a house as a machine for living.

All over Europe most artists of Kirchner's generation participated in the general cultural relaxation. Matisse and Kandinsky (who in 1924 were in their middle fifties) understandably experienced a mature mellowing of style in the 1920's and 1930's. But Picasso, Braque, and Klee in their early and mid-forties also produced works of remarkable calm when compared with some created but a few years earlier. These painters (among the most formally inventive of artists during the previous decade) dominated postwar formalist trends; Kirchner's work demands comparison with theirs. Their formal values are so central to European painting between the wars and so definitive of the entire artistic contribution of the generation born around 1880 that the very obviousness of these values should not lead us to overlook their basic significance. As Kirchner in Dresden had been the first German artist fundamentally to comprehend the pictorial revolution which had occurred on French soil just before and after 1900, so his Wildboden styles are the ones which invite comparison with those of Braque and Matisse in their central concern for *peinture pure.* And as Kirchner in the "Lärchen" years had attempted to wed inner fantasy with pictorial monumentality and decorative logic, so his eventual attainment of this goal at Wildboden— through relative independence from the object

—led him to achieve a glorification of fantasy in art such as that fully achieved at that time only by Picasso and Klee.

The Wildboden styles are tangentially related to those of these leading postwar painters (as the Dresden styles had been to postimpressionist and fauve artists): there is no real link to the contemporary German alternatives, classicism (verism) or "new objectivity," nor, given his basically realist intention to create a picture of his times, could Kirchner identify himself with international constructivist and non-objective trends or with the French surrealist direction. Instead, the Wildboden styles attain a unique decorative synthesis of abstract, expressive, sensuous, and representational forms. And one must thus look, for the key to the Wildboden development, to the *synthétiste* viewpoint propounded by French artists in the late nineteenth century. It is the synthetist aesthetic which subtly dominates the entire Wildboden period, especially in its last few years, when informed by a Rousseauean romanticism as appropriate to Alpine nature as it had once been to the exotic tropics. At Wildboden Kirchner pictorially realizes many implications of Gauguin's earlier formalist dream.

Although firmly rooted in his artistic origins, Kirchner's late styles remain boldly innovational to the end. Like Matisse, Braque, and Klee, who consolidated a single aesthetic viewpoint during these years, he retained that inner curiosity and formal inventeness which had characterized his work from its beginnings. Yet like his admired predecessor Albrecht Dürer, Kirchner displayed an ambivalent relation toward the dominant Latin artistic tradition of his time, to remain in some essentials an outsider. More like Picasso than any other contemporary artist, Kirchner at Wildboden ranged in temperament and in style from extremes of expression to those of abstraction, and from sheer decorative beauty to stunningly intuitive symbolic form.

Tapestries woven by Lise Gujer from Kirchner cartoons reinforce the abstractly decorative quality of the first Wildboden style. Visits by the Dresden art critic Will Grohmann lead to the first monographs on the artist in 1925 and 1926. 1924: forty-five works exhibited in Winterthur; visit by Rolf Nesch. 1925–26 (December-March): Kirchner's first German visit since 1917; monumental street scenes and city views of Frankfurt, Chemnitz, Dresden, and Berlin, executed upon his return to Wildboden. 1926: several paintings exhibited in Philadelphia and New York. Numerous exhibitions of his work in major German cities between 1923 and 1927.

A Wildboden Painting

The picture *Modern Bohemia* (Cat. no. 58), painted in 1924, is in the Minneapolis Institute of Arts. It depicts the interior of the Wildboden house in what might be called a "tapestry" style. Highly architectonic, it stresses rectangular shapes parallel to the picture frame and a strong emphasis upon vertical and horizontal compositional interrelations of figurative forms. The shapes comprising the nude figure on the left are noteworthy in this regard. Ostensibly forming a diagonal accent within the composition, the figure is yet subdivided into smaller forms largely rectangular in shape: the two upraised bent arms create a right-angled form keyed to the adjacent rectangular rug; the diagonals of the breasts emphasize the vertical and horizontal extension of the arms; and the lower thigh and both feet create horizontal accents paralleling those in the nearby rug pattern. Throughout the design, "horizontal" surfaces in nature are transformed into vertical pictorial planes, with precisely that naively conventional consistency which one encounters in Egyptian and Coptic art. The decorative unity of the whole is further enhanced by the fairly literal representation of large-figured rug and textile patterns in a manner not unlike Matisse at this time. Color too is modulated both in intensity and hue to give rich surface variety: the green wall, for example, varies from chartreuse on the left to bluer greens elsewhere, while the purple figure, upper left, is modulated between violet and intense red. The very brushstroke placements, in their horizontal and vertical variations, heighten the similarity of picture surface to textile weave.

In content this painting has generation-wide implications. That particular quality of postwar European intellectual life stressed here is the enforced isolation of each creative individual within an environment of highly enforced order. Although surrounded by books, flowers, *objets d'art,* each figure reads, writes, creates, or dreams in his own private and isolated world. For all of its compact order and sensuous appeal *Modern Bohemia,* in Kirchner's view, replaces the radical strivings of an earlier, emotionally intense and classless generation of artists with the dispassionate intellect of a more critical and less illusioned milieu. This is, to paraphrase Andrew Marvell, "a fine and private place / but none I think do there embrace."

Modern Bohemia (Bohême moderne), ca. 1924
The Minneapolis Institute of Arts (Bequest of Curt Valentin).

1927–1935

The abstract style, originating in synthetic cubist principle, Klee's autonomous line, and certain aspects of Coptic art, matures in paintings before 1930 and in color woodcuts from 1933. A personal parallel to the contemporary French *peinture pure,* these works transpose natural forms and relationships to arrive at an abstract, decorative, and imaginative synthesis. 1927–32: numerous brief visits to German cities; prolonged project for the decoration of the banquet hall in the Folkwang Museum, Essen (cancelled by the Nazi regime). Summer 1928: first painting shown at the Venice Biennale. Summer 1929: graphic works included in an exhibition at the Bibliothèque Nationale in Paris; visit by Fritz Winter. 1931: paintings included in exhibitions at the Museum of Modern Art, New York, and the Palace of Fine Arts, Brussels; elected to membership in the Prussian Academy, Berlin. 1933: 246 works exhibited at the Kunsthalle in Bern. 1934: visit by Schlemmer; first personal meeting with Klee in Bern. Autumn 1935: several severe illnesses.

1936–1938

Culminating in monumental landscapes from 1937 and 1938, the last style is representational and appears to be the product of renewed inner withdrawal. 1936: expectation of renewed war; Deutscher Künstlerbund dissolved by Nazi decree. 1937: first American retrospective exhibitions, in January at the Detroit Institute of Arts, and in the autumn at the Curt Valentin Gallery in New York; 639 Kirchner works confiscated from German public collections by the Nazis, of which thirty-two are shown in the "Degenerate Art" exhibition in Munich that summer (and in other German cities later). 1938: increasing illness and depression; suicide in Frauenkirch, June 15th.

A Late Painting

The magnificent landscapes of 1937 are stunning in their evocation of the timeless spirit of the Swiss mountainside in summer. One of them is *Sertig Path* (Cat. no. 68), in an American private collection. In this painting, beneath a darkly intense warm blue sky in which hover the pink and violet forms of a distant mountain peak, the eye travels down the forested green slopes, relieved here and there with phrased strokes in pure orange to suggest sunlight and larger patches of midnight blue shadow. In the valley itself the pure ultramarine shadows cast from the right along the irregularly sloping ground come into explosive contact with the lighter green and pure chartreuse of the grass in full sunlight. The tiny figures of a woman and a blond child in the foreground establish the monumental scale of the entire spatial vista, but the purity of all the colors creates a decorative harmony such that space and surface are one. The rhythmically meandering curves in both foreground and horizon add variety to a firmly structured composition dominated by the horizontals of houses, roofs, and lateral shadows, by the verticals of the tree trunks and by the carefully opposed diagonals of the major compositional masses.

The forms of paintings from 1937 and 1938 recall those of other artists trained in the impressionist generation: the landscapes are close to Hodler's; the figures incorporate the classicist "primeval innocence" of Böcklin (or even of Chavannes); and the architectonic pattern and rich color create tapestried surfaces not unlike those of Gauguin. Nowhere in the twentieth century outside of Wildboden do we find such analogues to the tradition of Gauguin and his time. What appears to have happened is that in his late fifties Kirchner withdrew into the private world of his own art, lost interest in the pictorial styles of contemporary Europe and of ancient, Oriental, and primitive sources, and gave disciplined expression to his most personal (and earliest) creative purpose. This purpose was, after all, decorative and representational rather than abstract. Or, more accurately, the purpose of art for Kirchner during more than three decades had been to discover pictorially logical methods with which to synthesize the existential freedom of the creative human imagination and the existential reality of a natural world which the human mind had had no part in making. Formalist in its most effective means, subjective in its most creative inspiration, this purpose could only result either in tension or conflict between what the late-nineteenth-century mind first saw as tragically irreconcilable opposites or, as now, in the idealistic resolution of these extremes through the power or grace of an inner or higher vision. Thus, in his last years Kirchner's idealism succeeded, not in escaping from reality, but in finally unifying self with world. It was a most appropriate world there at Wildboden—a corner of nature at the artist's doorstep among the most pantheistically awe-inspiring in Europe. But it was also now a most appropriate self—a temperament at twilight, as it were, finally free to relax its concern for contemporaneity and, amidst the gathering storm of renewed world self-destruction, to return to a nobler, simpler, and more universal vision.

68
Sertig Path (Sertigweg), ca. 1937
Mr. and Mrs. Stephen Adler, Holliswood, New York.

Catalogue

Paintings

Dates following the titles are given on the
basis of stylistic or documentary evidence
and may differ from the date that appears on
the work. In the dimensions height precedes
width.

1
Woman Embroidering (Stickende Frau),
ca. 1904–05
Oil on board. 9³/₄ x 13⁷/₈ in.
Signed and dated, lower right:
E. L. Kirchner 98
Collection: Kirchner Estate
Lender: Dr. Ulrich Kirchner, Biberach/Riss

Reference: D. Gordon, *Kirchner,* 1968, no. 4.
Exhibitions: Dresden, Sächsischer Kunstverein, 1907; Hamburg, Hannover, Bremen,
Wuppertal-Elberfeld, *Kirchner, Werke aus
dem Nachlass,* 1950–51, no. 1; Zürich, Kunsthaus, *Kirchner,* 1952, no. 2; Saulgau/Württem-
berg, Museum Die Fähre, *Von Corinth bis
Antes,* 1964.

2
Erich Heckel and Model in Studio
(Erich Heckel und Modell im Atelier), 1905
Oil on board. 19⁵/₈ x 13¹/₄ in.
Signed and dated, lower right:
E. L. Kirchner 05
Collection: Lise Gujer, Davos
Lender: E. W. Kornfeld, Bern

Reference: D. Gordon, *Kirchner,* 1968, no. 6
(pl. 3).

3
Lake in Dresden Park (Morgen am Teich),
1906
Oil on board. 20¹/₂ x 27¹/₂ in.
Signed and dated, lower left:
E. L. Kirchner 06
Collections: Kirchner Estate; E. Teltsch
London
Lenders: Mr. and Mrs. Ernest Gottlieb,
New York
(Boston only)

References: W. Grohmann, *E. L. Kirchner,*
1958, (repr. p. 9, color); D. Gordon, "Kirchner
in Dresden," *Art Bulletin,* XLVIII, nos. 3–4,
1966, (fig. 1); D. Gordon, *Kirchner,* 1968, no. 13
(pl. 4).
Exhibitions: Essen, Museum Folkwang,
Brücke 1905–1913, 1958, no. 56; Ulm,
Museum, Brücke, 1959, no. 1; Bremen,
Hannover, The Hague, Cologne, Zürich,
*Meisterwerke des deutschen Expressionis-
mus,* 1960–61, no. 4 (repr., color); Florence,
Palazzo Strozzi, *"L'espressionismo: pittura,
scultura, architettura,"* 1964, no. 171 (repr.);
London, Tate Gallery, *Painters of the
"Brücke,"* 1964, no. 55; New York, Leonard
Hutton Galleries, *Fauves and Expressionists,*
1968, no. 46 (repr. p. 49, color).

4
Child's Head (Kinderköpfchen), 1906
Oil on board. 18⁷/₈ x 19¹/₂ in.
Signed and dated, lower right:
E. L. Kirchner 06
Lender: Galerie Wolfgang Ketterer, Munich

Reference: D. Gordon, *Kirchner,* 1968, no. 18
(pl. 5).
Exhibition: Paris, Musée National d'Art
Moderne and Munich, Haus der Kunst, *Le
fauvisme français et les debuts de l'expressionisme allemand,* 1966.

5
Girl on a Divan (Mädchen auf dem Diwan),
ca. 1906
Oil on board. 19¹/₄ x 27¹/₄ in.
Signed and dated, lower left:
E. L. Kirchner, 06
Collection: Kirchner Estate
Lenders: Mr. and Mrs. Ernest Gottlieb,
New York
(Boston only)

Reference: D. Gordon, *Kirchner,* 1968, no. 20
(pl. II, color).
Exhibitions: Bremen, Hannover, The Hague,
Cologne, Zürich, *Meisterwerke des deut-
schen Expressionismus,* 1960–61, no. 6;
Campione, Galerie R. N. Ketterer, *Moderne
Kunst,* 1963, (repr., color); New York, Leonard
Hutton Galleries, *Fauves and Expressionists,*
1968, no. 47 (repr. p. 31, color).

6
Landscape, Road with Trees
(Landschaft, Weg mit Bäumen), ca. 1907
Oil on board. 13³/₄ x 8¹/₈ in.
Collection: Erna Kirchner, Frauenkirch
Lender: Rätus Kern, Zürich, Switzerland

Reference: D. Gordon, *Kirchner,* 1968, no. 25
(pl. 7).

Portrait of the Painter Heckel, ca. 1907
Oil on board. 27$^1/_2$ x 19$^7/_8$ in.
Collection: Kirchner Estate
Lender: Anonymous loan

References: H. Wentzel, *Bildnisse Brücke-*
Künstler voneinander, 1961, (fig. 2); D. Gor-
don, *Kirchner,* 1968, no. 28 (pl. 8).
Exhibitions: Düsseldorf, Kunsthalle, *Kirch-*
ner, 1960, no. 1 (repr.); London, Tate Gallery,
Painters of the "Brücke," 1964, no. 56 (repr.).

8

Man Resting, Portrait of Hans Frisch
(Ruhender Mann, Hans Frisch), ca. 1907
Color plate: p. 19
Oil on canvas. 45 x 45 in.
Collections: Kirchner Estate; Walter Bareiss,
Greenwich, Connecticut
Lender: Marion Koogler McNay Art Institute,
San Antonio

References: D. Gordon, "Kirchner in Dres-
den," *Art Bulletin,* XLVIII, nos. 3–4, 1966,
p. 343; D. Gordon, *Kirchner,* 1968, no. 33
(pl. III, color).
Exhibitions: St. Gallen, Kunstmuseum, *Kirch-
ner,* 1950, no. 4; Stuttgart, Württembergischer
Kunstverein, *Kirchner,* 1956, no. 2; New York,
Fine Arts Associates, *Kirchner,* 1957, no. 3
(repr.); Raleigh, North Carolina Museum of
Art, *Kirchner,* 1958, no. 1 (repr.); Düsseldorf,
Kunsthalle, *Kirchner,* 1960, no. 5 (repr.); New
Haven, Yale University Art Gallery, *Paintings,
Drawings, and Sculptures Collected by Yale
Alumni,* 1960, no. 119 (repr.).

9

Emmy Frisch with Red Flowers
(Emmy Frisch mit roten Blumen), ca. 1908
Oil on canvas. 59^1/$_8$ x 28^7/$_8$ in.
Collections: Kirchner Estate; William
S. Rubin, New York
Lender: The Museum of Modern Art, New
York (Gift of William S. Rubin)

References: *The Museum of Modern Art
Bulletin,* XXIV, no. 4, 1957, no. 1277 (repr.);
The Museum of Modern Art Catalogue, 1958,
p. 33; D. Gordon, *Kirchner,* 1968, no. 35
(pl. 10).
Exhibitions: Cambridge, Mass., Busch-
Reisinger Museum, *Kirchner,* 1950–51; New
York, Curt Valentin Gallery, *Kirchner,* 1952,
no. 1.

10

Fehmarn Houses (Fehmarn-Häuser), 1908
Oil on canvas. 29^1/$_2$ x 38^5/$_8$ in.
Signed and dated, lower left:
E. L. Kirchner 08
Collections: Hahn collection, Berlin; Dr. Carl
Hagemann, Frankfurt am Main
Lender: Anonymous loan

References: B. Myers, "Ernst Ludwig
Kirchner and 'Die Brücke'," *Magazine of Art,*
XLV, no. 1, 1952, (repr. p. 21); B. Myers, *The
German Expressionists,* 1957, p. 126; D. Gor-
don, *Kirchner,* 1968, no. 37 (pl. 11).
Exhibitions: Dresden, Kunstsalon Richter,
Brücke, 1908; Frankfurt am Main, Städtische
Galerie, 1948; Essen, Museum Folkwang,
Brücke, 1905–13, 1958, no. 64; Düsseldorf,
Kunsthalle, *Kirchner,* 1960, no. 2 (repr.);
Schleswig, Landesmuseum and Lübeck,
Overbeck-Gesellschaft, *Die Maler der
"Brücke,"* 1962, no. 21.

There is a drawing of the same subject in
brush and ink in the Kirchner Estate and an
etching, reversed (Dube 47).

11

Dodo and Her Brother

(Dodo und ihr Bruder), ca. 1908
Oil on canvas. 67 1/8 x 37 in.
Signed, lower left: *E. L. Kirchner*
Collection: Kirchner Estate
Lender: Smith College Museum of Art,
Northampton, Massachusetts

References: L. Buchheim, *Die Künstlergemeinschaft Brücke,* 1956 (fig. 158); *Art
News,* LV, no. 3, 1956, p. 5 (repr. cover,
color); *The Art Quarterly,* XIX, no. 2, 1956
(repr. p. 204); R. Parks, "Kirchner's Portrait
of the Heckels," *College Art Journal,* XV,
no. 3, 1956, p. 184 (repr. cover); *Sele Arte,*
Sept.–Oct., 1956 (repr.); *Smith Alumnae
Quarterly,* Winter, 1956, p. 86; P. Selz, *German Expressionist Painting,* 1957, p. 103 (pl.
147, color); B. Myers, "Kirchner's Dodo and
Her Brother," *Smith College Museum of Art
Bulletin,* 37, 1957, pp. 21–26 (fig. 10); D. Gordon, "Kirchner in Dresden," *Art Bulletin,*
XLVIII, nos. 3–4, 1966, (fig. 25); E. Bryant,
"The Boom in U. S. University Museums,"
Art News, LXVI, no. 5, 1967 (repr. p. 44,
color); D. Gordon, *Kirchner,* 1968, no. 48
(pl. 13).

Exhibitions: St. Gallen, Kunstmuseum, *Kirchner,* 1950, no. 5; Basel, Galerie Beyeler, *Expressionisten,* 1955, no. 16 (repr.); New York,
The Museum of Modern Art and St. Louis,
City Art Museum, *German Art of the Twentieth Century,* 1957–58, no. 70 (repr.); The
Cleveland Museum of Art, *Paths of Abstract
Art,* 1960, no. 14 (repr.); Chicago, The Arts
Club, *Smith College Loan Exhibition,* 1961,
no. 13 (repr.); Wellesley College, Mass.,
Jewett Arts Center, *Painting and Sculpture
in Europe and America from 1900–1914,*
1963; New York, The Solomon R. Guggen-
heim Museum, *Van Gogh and Expressionism
in Modern Art,* 1964; New York, Public
Education Association, *Seven Decades of
Modern Art (1895–1965),* 1966, no. 72 (repr.);
Amherst College, Mass., *German Art after
World War I,* 1966.

12

Street, Dresden (Strasse, Dresden), ca. 1908
Oil on canvas. 59 x 79 in.
Signed and dated, lower left: *E.L.Kirchner 07*
Collection: Kirchner Estate
Lender: The Museum of Modern Art, New York

References: W. Grohmann, *Das Werk Ernst
Ludwig Kirchners,* 1926, no.18; *Werk,* XXXV,
no.1, 1948, (repr. p.20); M. Raynal *et al.,
Geschichte der modernen Malerei; Fauvis-
mus und Expressionismus,* 1950–51, II, (repr.
p.82, color); B. Myers, "Ernst Ludwig
Kirchner and 'Die Brücke,'" *Magazine of Art,*
XLV, no.1, 1952, (repr. p.21); *The Museum of
Modern Art Bulletin,* XIV, no.3, 1952, no.943
(repr.); L. Buchheim, *Die Künstlergemein-
schaft Brücke,* 1956, (fig.142, color);
B. Myers, *The German Expressionists,* 1957,
p.126 (fig.25); P. Selz, *German Expressionist
Painting,* 1957, pp.102–03 (fig.28); E. Roters,
"Beiträge zur Geschichte der Künstlergruppe
'Brücke' in den Jahren 1905–1907," *Jahrbuch
der Berliner Museen,* II, 1960, pp.172–210
(repr. p.202); W. Grohmann, *E. L. Kirchner,*
1961, (repr. p.15, color; p.105); W. Haftmann,
Malerei im 20. Jahrhundert, 1962, II, (repr.
p.90); D. Gordon, "Kirchner in Dresden,"
Art Bulletin, XLVIII, nos.3–4, 1966, p.346;
D. Gordon, *Kirchner,* 1968, no.53 (pl.14).
Exhibitions: Winterthur, Kunstverein, *Kirch-
ner,* 1924, no.9; Bern, Kunsthalle, *Kirchner,*
1933, no.8; Bern, Kunsthalle, *Paula Moder-
sohn und die Maler der "Brücke,"* 1948,
no.49; Cambridge, Mass., Busch-Reisinger
Museum, *Kirchner,* 1950–51; New York, Curt
Valentin Gallery, *Kirchner,* 1952, no.2 (repr.);
Buffalo, Albright Art Gallery, *Fifty Paintings,
1905–1913,* 1955, no.25 (repr. p.47); Raleigh,
North Carolina Museum of Art, *Kirchner,*
1958, no.8 (repr.); Düsseldorf, Kunsthalle,
Kirchner, 1960, no.8 (repr.).
Kirchner dates the painting both "1908" and
"1907" in a letter to Prof. Will Grohmann,
December 2, 1925. He mentions "thorough
restoration" of the painting in his diary,
p.76, October 6 and 7, 1919. Lithograph of
the same subject, reversed (Dube 55) in this
exhibition, Cat. no.112.

13
Reclining Nude (Liegender Akt), 1909
Oil on canvas. 29³/₈ x 59¹/₂ in.
Signed and dated, lower left:
E. L. Kirchner 09
Collections: Elisabeth Ris, Zürich-Küss-
nacht; Dr. Hermann Ganz, Zürich
Lender: Museum of Fine Arts, Boston
(Arthur Gordon Tompkins Residuary Fund)

References: Museum of Fine Arts, Boston,
Bulletin, LVIII, nos. 313–14, 1960, (repr.
p. 101); D. Gordon, *Kirchner,* 1968, no. 55
(pl. 17).
Exhibitions: Zürich, Kunststube im Rösslyn,
E. L. Kirchner und sein Kreis, 1943, no. 189;
Colorado Springs Fine Arts Center, *New
Accessions USA,* 1958, no. 5 (repr.); Colum-
bus, Ohio, Gallery of Fine Arts, *German
Expressionism,* 1961, no. 30; Pasadena Art
Museum, *German Expressionism,* 1961,
no. 43; London, Tate Gallery, *Painters of the
"Brücke,"* 1964, no. 59.

14

Girl under Japanese Umbrella
(Mädchen unter Japanschirm), ca. 1909
Oil on canvas. $36^{1}/_{4}$ x $31^{1}/_{2}$ in.
Signed and dated, lower right: *E. L. Kirchner 06*
Collection: Dr. Frederic Bauer, Davos
Lender: Kunstsammlung Nordrhein-Westfalen, Düsseldorf
(Boston only)

References: U. Apollonio, *"Die Brücke" e la cultura dell'espressionismo*, 1952, (fig. 10); W. Grohmann, *E. L. Kirchner*, 1958, (repr. p. 13, color); D. Gordon, "Kirchner in Dresden," *Art Bulletin*, XLVIII, nos. 3–4, 1966, (figs. 2, 3); D. Gordon, *Kirchner*, 1968, no. 57 (pl. V, color).
Exhibitions: Bern, Kunsthalle, *Kirchner*, 1933, no. 3; Bern, Kunsthalle, *Paula Modersohn und die Maler der "Brücke,"* 1948, no. 48; Nuremberg, Munich, Freiburg, Mannheim, Berlin, *Sammlung Dr. F. Bauer, Davos*, 1952, no. 1 (repr.); Stuttgart, Württembergischer Kunstverein, *Kirchner*, 1956, no. 3, (repr., color); Essen, Museum Folkwang, *Brücke, 1905–1913*, 1958, no. 55 (repr.); Berlin-Charlottenburg, Orangerie, *Triumph der Farbe*, 1959, no. 81; Ulm, Museum, *Brücke*, 1959, no. 3; Bremen, Hannover, The Hague, Cologne, Zürich, *Meisterwerke des deutschen Expressionismus*, 1960–61, no. 12 (repr., color).

15
Landscape in Spring (Frühlingslandschaft),
ca. 1909
Oil on canvas. 27³/₄ x 35⁵/₈ in.
Signed, center bottom: *E. L. Kirchner*
Collection: Max Gläser, Kaiserslautern
Lender: Pfalzgalerie, Kaiserslautern

References: D. Gordon, "Kirchner in Dresden," *Art Bulletin,* XLVIII, nos. 3–4, 1966,
p. 350 (fig. 37); D. Gordon, *Kirchner,* 1968,
no. 62 (pl. 18).
Exhibitions: Dresden, Kunstsalon Richter,
Brücke, 1909; Basel, Kunsthalle, *E. L. Kirchner und Rot-Blau,* 1967.

16
Japanese Theater (Japanisches Theater),
ca. 1909
Oil on canvas. 45¹/₄ x 45 in.
Collections: Kirchner Estate; Hugo Gouthier,
Brazilian Ambassador at Rome.
Lender: Scottish National Gallery of Modern
Art, Edinburgh

References: *Burlington Magazine,* CVII,
no. 750, 1965, (repr. p. 491); National Galleries of Scotland, *Poster-Bulletin,* 1965,
no. 2; "La chronique des arts," *Gazette des
beaux arts,* February 1966, p. 81, no. 310;
D. Gordon, *Kirchner,* 1968, no. 69 (pl. 19).
Exhibition: London, Tate Gallery, *Painters
of the "Brücke,"* 1964, no. 61.

17
Wrestlers in a Circus
(Ringkämpfer im Zirkus), ca. 1909
Oil on canvas. 31³/₄ x 37 in.
Signed, lower left: *E L Kirchner*
Collection: Kirchner Estate
Lender: Contemporary Collection of The
Cleveland Museum of Art (Bequest of
William R. Valentiner)

References: W. Grohmann, *Das Werk Ernst
Ludwig Kirchners,* 1926, (fig. 13); The
Cleveland Museum of Art, *Bulletin,* LIII,
no. 7, 1966, pp. 240–41 (fig. 117); E. Henning,
"German Expressionist Paintings in the
Cleveland Museum of Art," *Burlington
Magazine,* CVIII, no. 765, 1966, p. 633 (repr.
p. 632); D. Gordon, *Kirchner,* 1968, no. 70
(pl. 20).
Exhibitions: Frankfurt am Main, Galerie Lud-
wig Schames, *Kirchner,* 1919, no. 41; Zürich,
Kunsthaus, *Kirchner,* 1952, no. 6; New York,
Fine Arts Associates, *Kirchner,* 1957, no. 4;
New York, Marlborough-Gerson Gallery, *A
Tribute to Curt Valentin,* 1963, no. 251 (repr.);
New York, The Solomon R. Guggenheim Mu-
seum, *Van Gogh and Expressionism in
Modern Art,* 1964; The Cleveland Museum of
Art, *Golden Anniversary Acquisitions,* 1966.

8
Four Bathers (Vier Badende), ca. 1909
Oil on canvas. $35^{1}/_{2}$ x $39^{5}/_{8}$ in.
Collection: Baron Eduard von der Heydt,
Wuppertal
Lender: Von der Heydt Museum der Stadt
Wuppertal

Reference: D. Gordon, *Kirchner,* 1968, no. 95
(pl. 23).
Exhibition: Bern, Kunsthalle, *Paula Modersohn und die Maler der "Brücke,"* 1948,
no. 55.

52

19
Fränzi in Carved Chair
(Fränzi vor geschnitztem Stuhl), ca. 1910
Oil on canvas. 27³/₄ x 19³/₄ in.
Signed, lower right: *E. L. Kirchner*
Collection: Kirchner Estate
Lender: Collection Thyssen Bornemisza,
Lugano-Castagnola, Switzerland

References: *Kunst und Künstler,* XVIII, no. 5,
1920, p. 217; W. Grohmann, *E. L. Kirchner,*
1961, (repr. p. 17, color); D. Gordon, *Kirchner,*
1968, no. 122 (pl. VII, color).
Exhibitions: Essen, Museum Folkwang,
Brücke, 1905–1913, 1958, no. 60; Munich,
Galerie Günther Franke, *Bildnisse der ersten
Hälfte des 20. Jahrhunderts;* Ulm, Museum,
Brücke, 1959, no. 5; Bremen, Hannover, The
Hague, Cologne, Zürich, *Meisterwerke des
deutschen Expressionismus,* 1960–61, no. 13
(repr., color); London, Tate Gallery, *Painters
of the "Brücke,"* 1964, no. 63 (pl. 23); Lau-
sanne, Palais Beaulieu, Exposition Nationale
Suisse, *Chef d'œuvres des collections
suisses de Manet à Picasso,* 1964, no. 187
(repr.).
There is a pastel of the same subject in the
Städelsches Kunstinstitut in Frankfurt.

20
Seated Girl, Fränzi
(Sitzendes Mädchen, Fränzi), ca. 1910
Oil on canvas 31¼ x 35¼ in.
Collection: Kirchner Estate
Lender: The Minneapolis Institute of Arts

References: W. Grohmann, *Das Werk Ernst Ludwig Kirchners,* 1926, no. 16; M. Raynal *et al., Geschichte der modernen Malerei; Fauvismus und Expressionismus,* 1950–51, II, (repr. p. 83, color); The Minneapolis Institute of Arts, *Bulletin,* XLII, no. 6, 1953, pp. 26–29; L. Buchheim, *Die Künstlergemeinschaft Brücke,* 1956, (fig. 148, color); B. Myers, *The German Expressionists,* 1957, pp. 126–28; P. Selz, *German Expressionist Painting,* 1957, p. 112; *Scala International,* no. 2, 1961, p. 5 (repr. p. 24, color); *European Paintings in the Minneapolis Institute of Arts,* 1963, p. 81; D. Gordon, *Kirchner,* 1968, no. 123 (pl. 27).
Exhibitions: Bern, Kunsthalle, *Les Fauves und die Zeitgenossen,* 1950, no. 141; Hamburg, Hannover, Bremen, Wuppertal-Elberfeld, *Kirchner, Werke aus dem Nachlass,* 1950–51, no. 9 (repr.); New York, Curt Valentin Gallery, *Kirchner,* 1952, no. 3 (repr.); New York, Curt Valentin Gallery, *Curt Valentin Memorial Exhibition,* 1954; Raleigh, North Carolina Museum of Art, *Kirchner,* 1958, no. 10 (repr.); Columbus, Ohio, Gallery of Fine Arts, *German Expressionism,* 1961, no. 29.

21
Red Houses, Red January II
(Rote Häuser, Roter Januar II), ca. 1910
Oil on canvas. 29¹/₂ x 35³/₄ in.
Collection: Kunsthalle, Mannheim
Lender: Kurt H. Grunebaum, Harrison,
New York

References: F. Roh, *"Entartete" Kunst;
Kunstbarbarei im dritten Reich,* 1962, p. 214;
D. Gordon, *Kirchner,* 1968, no. 128 (pl. 28).

22
Windmill (Windmühle), ca. 1910
Oil on canvas. 31⁷/₈ x 27⁵/₈ in.
Signed, lower right: *E. L. Kirchner*
Collection: Dr. O. Binswanger, Kreuzlingen
Lender: E. W. Kornfeld, Bern

Reference: D. Gordon, *Kirchner,* 1968,
no. 131.
Exhibition: Düsseldorf, Kunsthalle, *Kirchner,*
1960, no. 11 (repr.).

23
Road through a Wood (Waldstrasse), ca. 1910
Oil on canvas. $31^7/_8$ x 28 in.
Signed, lower right: *E. L. Kirchner*
Collection: Hede Vasen, Carmel
Lender: Dr. Arthur Weisz, New York
(Boston only)

Reference: D. Gordon, *Kirchner,* 1968,
no. 136.
Exhibitions: Dresden, Galerie Arnold,
Brücke, 1910, no. 32; London, Tate Gallery,
Painters of the "Brücke," 1964, no. 82.

24
Panama Girls (Panamatänzerinnen), ca. 1910
Oil on canvas. 19³/₄ x 19³/₄ in.
Signed, lower right: *E. . . Kirchner 19 . .* (10?)
Collection: Wilhelm R. Valentiner, Raleigh
Lender: North Carolina Museum of Art,
Raleigh (Bequest of Wilhelm R. Valentiner)

References: *The Art Quarterly,* XXVI, no. 2,
1963, p. 275; D. Gordon, *Kirchner,* 1968,
no. 161 (pl. 30).
Exhibitions: Los Angeles, Paul Kantor Gallery, *Kirchner,* 1957, no. 4; Raleigh, North
Carolina Museum of Art, *Kirchner,* 1958.
no. 12 (repr.); Raleigh, North Carolina Museum of Art, *Masterpieces of Art,* 1959,
no. 130 (repr.); Detroit, J. L. Hudson Gallery,
The W. R. Valentiner Memorial Exhibition,
1963–64, no. 20.
A pen and ink drawing of the same subject
is reproduced in *Der Sturm,* April 29, 1911,
p. 483.

25
Dodo Nude against Blue Background
(Dodo Akt vor blauem Grund), ca. 1911
Oil on canvas. 31³/₄ x 27⁵/₈ in.
Signed, lower left: *E. L. Kirchner*
Lender: Lothar Günther Buchheim, Feldafing

Reference: D. Gordon, *Kirchner,* 1968,
no. 182.
Exhibitions: Munich, Sammlung Buchheim,
Die Maler der Brücke, 1959, no 2 (repr.,
color); Tokyo, *Der Deutsche Expressionismus,* 1963, no. 29; Paris, Musée National
d'Art Moderne and Munich, Haus der Kunst,
*Le fauvisme français et les débuts de
l'expressionisme allemand,* 1966, no. 201
(pl. 277); Basel, Kunsthalle, *E. L. Kirchner
und Rot-Blau,* 1967, no. 19 (repr., color).

26
Portrait of a Woman (Frauenbildnis), 1911
Oil on canvas. 47 x 35 in.
Signed and dated, lower right:
E. L. Kirchner 11
Collection: Kirchner Estate
Lender: Albright-Knox Art Gallery, Buffalo

References: P. Selz, *German Expressionist
Painting,* 1957, p. 138 (pl. 155, color); *The Art
Quarterly,* XX, no. 3, 1957, p. 324 (repr.
p. 326); *Gallery Notes,* XXI, no. 1, 1958,
(repr. p. 2); D. Gordon, *Kirchner,* 1968,
no. 185 (pl. 36).
Exhibition: Claremont, Berkeley, Santa
Barbara, *German Expressionist Painting,*
1957–58, no. 22 (repr., color).

27
Otto and Maschka Müller in the Studio
(Otto und Maschka Müller im Atelier),
ca. 1911
Oil on canvas. $44^{1}/_{2}$ x 24 in.
Collection: Rosi Fischer, Frankfurt am Main
Lenders: Dr. and Mrs. Ernst Fischer, Albany

Reference: D. Gordon, *Kirchner,* 1968,
no. 197.
Exhibitions: Frankfurt am Main, Galerie
Ludwig Schames, *Kirchner,* 1919, no. 43;
Raleigh, North Carolina Museum of Art,
Kirchner, 1958, no. 16 (repr.); Norfolk (Va.)
Museum, *German Expressionism,* 1960,
no. 24 (repr.).

28
Lake in Bohemian Forest (Böhmerwaldsee),
ca. 1911
Oil on canvas. $31^3/_4 \times 35^3/_4$ in.
Signed, lower left: *E. L. Kirchner*
Collection: Dr. Frederic Bauer, Davos
Lender: Bayerische Staatsgemäldesamm-
lungen, Munich

References: U. Apollonio, *"Die Brücke" e la
cultura dell'espressionismo*, 1952, p. 15
(repr.); L. Buchheim, *Die Künstlergemeinschaft Brücke*, 1956, (fig. 160); D. Gordon,
Kirchner, 1968, no. 199.
Exhibitions: Nuremberg, Munich, Freiburg,
Mannheim, Berlin, *Sammlung Dr. F. Bauer,
Davos*, 1952–53, no. 3 (repr.); Essen,
Museum Folkwang, *Brücke, 1905–1913*,
1958, no. 63; Munich, Neue Pinakothek/Neue
Staatsgalerie, *Französische Meister des
19. Jahrhunderts/Kunst des 20. Jahrhunderts*,
1966, p. 52 (repr.).

29
Russian Girl (Die Russin), 1912
Oil on canvas. 59⅛ x 29¾ in.
Signed and dated, lower right: *E L Kirch-*
ner 12
Collections: Museum, Magdeburg; Dr. Josef
Haubrich, Cologne
Lender: Wallraf-Richartz-Museum, Cologne

References: G. Händler, *Deutsche Malerei*
der Gegenwart, 1956, (fig. 3); L. Buchheim,
Die Künstlergemeinschaft Brücke, 1956,
(fig. 171); D. Gordon, *Kirchner,* 1968, no. 228.
Exhibitions: Zürich, Kunsthaus, *Kirchner,*
1952, no. 28; Turin, Museo Civico, *Espres-*
sionismo e arte tedesca del 20° secolo,
1954; São Paulo, V. Bienal do Museu de Arte
Moderna, 1959, no. 4 (repr.).

30
Staberhuk Beacon, Fehmarn
(Leuchtturm Staberhuk, Fehmarn), 1912
Oil on canvas. 46 x 35 in.
Signed and dated, lower right: *E. L. Kirch-*
ner 12
Collection: Kirchner Estate
Lender: Museum of Art, Carnegie Institute,
Pittsburgh

References: *Carnegie Magazine,* June, 1965;
D. Gordon, *Kirchner,* 1968, no. 252 (pl. 41).

31
Bather between Rocks
(Badende zwischen Steinen), ca. 1912
Oil on canvas. 18 x 23¾ in.
Collection: Frau Irene Eucken, Jena
Lender: Frau Edith Eucken-Erdsiek, Freiburg

Reference: D. Gordon, *Kirchner,* 1968, no. 256
(pl. 42).

32

Striding into the Sea (Ins Meer Schreitende),
ca. 1912
Oil on canvas. $57^3/_4$ x $78^3/_4$ in.
Signed, lower right: *E. L. Kirchner*
Collections: Rosi Fischer, Frankfurt am
Main; Museum, Halle; Baron Philippe Lam-
bert, Brussels; E. G. Bührle, Zürich
Lender: Staatsgalerie, Stuttgart

References: *Cicerone,* XVII, no. 20, 1925,
(repr. p. 975); W. Grohmann, *E. L. Kirchner,*
1961, (repr. p. 119); D. Gordon, *Kirchner,*
1968, no. 262 (pl. X, color).
Exhibitions: Essen, Museum Folkwang,
Brücke, 1905–1913, 1958, no. 85; London,
Marlborough Fine Art Ltd., *Art in Revolt;
Germany, 1905–1925,* 1959, no. 10; Munich,
Haus der Kunst, *Entartete Kunst; Bildersturm
vor 25 Jahren,* 1962, no. 64 (repr.); London,
Tate Gallery, *Painters of the "Brücke,"* 1964,
no. 73.

33
Still Life with Pitcher (Stilleben mit Krug),
ca. 1912
Oil on canvas. 31³/₄ x 28¹/₈ in.
Signed, lower right: *E L Kirchner*
Collections: Baron August von der Heydt,
Wuppertal; Baron Eduard von der Heydt,
Wuppertal
Lender: Von der Heydt Museum der Stadt
Wuppertal

Reference: D. Gordon, *Kirchner,* 1968,
no. 283 (pl. 43).

34
Portrait of Dr. Alfred Döblin, 1912
Oil on canvas. 20 x 16¼ in.
Signed and dated, lower left: *E. L. Kirchner*
Collections: Rosi Fischer, Frankfurt am
Main; Gustav Kauner, Berlin
Lender: Busch-Reisinger Museum, Harvard
University

References: P. Selz, *German Expressionist
Painting,* 1957, p. 299 (fig. 137); C. Kuhn and
J. Rosenberg, *German Expressionism and
Abstract Art; The Harvard Collections,* 1957,
p. 51 (fig. 8); D. Gordon, *Kirchner,* 1968,
no. 290 (pl. 45).
Exhibitions: Frankfurt am Main, Galerie
Ludwig Schames, *Kirchner,* 1916, no. 8;
Cambridge, Mass., Busch-Reisinger Museum,
Kirchner, 1950–51.
There is a lithograph of the same subject,
reversed (Dube 223).

35
Street in Schöneberg City Park,
Innsbruck Street
(Strasse am Stadtpark Schöneberg,
Innsbrucker Strasse), ca. 1912–13
Oil on canvas. 47³/₄ x 59¹/₂ in.
Signed, lower left: E L Kirchner
Collections: Dr. Hans Koch, Randegg, Ger-
many; Harry Lynde Bradley, Milwaukee
Lender: Milwaukee Art Center (Gift of
Mrs. Harry Lynde Bradley)

References: W. Grohmann, *E. L. Kirchner,*
1961, (repr. p. 49, color); D. Gordon,
Kirchner, 1968, no. 292 (pl. 46).
Exhibitions: Berlin, Freie Sezession, 1914,
no. 108; Frankfurt am Main, Galerie Ludwig
Schames, *Kirchner,* 1919, no. 46 (repr.);
Zürich, Kunsthaus, *Kirchner,* 1952, no. 35;
Essen, Museum Folkwang, *Brücke, 1905–*
1913, 1958, no. 88; Stuttgart, Staatsgalerie,
Brücke, 1959, (pl. 13); Ulm, Museum, *Die*
Brücke, 1959, no. 10; Bremen, Hannover,
The Hague, Cologne, Zürich, *Meisterwerke*
des deutschen Expressionismus, 1960–61,
no. 20 (repr., color); Milwaukee Art Center,
Bradley Collection, 1962, no. 53.

36
Otto Müller with Pipe
(Otto Müller mit Pfeife), ca. 1913
Oil on canvas. 23¹/₂ x 19¹/₄ in.
Signed, upper right: *E. L. Kirchner*
Collection: Dr. L. Binswanger, Kreuzlingen
Lender: E. W. Kornfeld, Bern

Reference: D. Gordon, *Kirchner,* 1968,
no. 296 (pl. 47).
Exhibition: Basel, Kunsthalle, *E. L. Kirchner*
und Rot-Blau, 1967.

37
Sick Woman, Woman with Hat
(Kranke Frau, Dame mit Hut), ca. 1913
Oil on canvas. 28$\frac{1}{8}$ x 23$\frac{7}{8}$ in.
Signed, upper left: *E L Kirchner*
Collection: Dr. Carl Hagemann, Frankfurt am
Main
Lender: Karlheinz Gabler, Frankfurt am Main

References: W. Grohmann, *Das Werk Ernst
Ludwig Kirchners,* 1926, (pl. 1, color);
B. Myers, *The German Expressionists,* 1957,
pp. 25, 128, 130 (fig. 134); P. Selz, *German
Expressionist Painting,* 1957, p. 138 (fig. 48);
W. Grohmann, *E. L. Kirchner,* 1961, (repr.
p. 37, color); D. Gordon, *Kirchner,* 1968,
no. 298 (pl. 48).
Exhibitions: Venice, XXVI Biennale, *Brücke,*
1952; Kassel, Museum Fridericianum,
Documenta I; Kunst des 20. Jahrhunderts,
1955, no. 264; Essen, Museum Folkwang,
Brücke, 1905–1913, 1958, no. 83 (repr.); Paris,
Musée National d'Art Moderne, *Les sources
du XXe siècle,* 1960–61, no. 299; Darmstadt,
Zeugnisse der Angst in der modernen Kunst,
1963, (pl. 119, color); Frankfurt am Main,
Kunstverein, *Moderne Malerei im Frankfurter
Privatbesitz,* 1963, (repr., color); London,
Tate Gallery, *Painters of the "Brücke,"* 1964,
no. 77; Basel, Kunsthalle, *E. L. Kirchner und
Rot-Blau,* 1967.

38
Staberhof Countryseat, Fehmarn I
(Gut Staberhof, Fehmarn I), 1913
Oil on canvas. 47⅝ x 59⅝ in.
Signed, lower right: *E. L. Kirchner*
Collection: Städtische Galerie,
Frankfurt am Main
Lender: Hamburger Kunsthalle

References: *Jahrbuch Hamburger Kunst-*
sammlungen, II, 1952, p. 16; W. Grohmann,
E. L. Kirchner, 1961, (repr. p. 120); F. Roh,
"Entartete" Kunst; Kunstbarbarei im dritten
Reich, 1962, p. 185; W. Haftmann, *Malerei im*
20. Jahrhundert, 1962, II, (repr. p. 80); D. Gor-
don, *Kirchner,* 1968, no. 322 (pl. 51).
Exhibitions: Berlin, Landesausstellungs-
Gebäude, 1919; Frankfurt am Main, Galerie
Ludwig Schames, *Kirchner,* 1919, no. 18;
Stuttgart, *Ausstellung neuer deutscher Kunst,*
1924, no. 81; London, Tate Gallery, *A Hundred*
Years of German Painting, 1956, no. 73;
Essen, Museum Folkwang, *Brücke, 1905–*
1913, no. 81; Düsseldorf, Kunsthalle, *Kirchner,*
1960, no. 38 (repr.); Paris, Musée National
d'Art Moderne, *Les sources du XXe siècle,*
1960–61, no. 301; Schleswig, Landesmuseum
and Lübeck, Overbeck-Gesellschaft, *Die*
Maler der "Brücke," 1962, no. 22.
Werner Gothein mentions paintings of this
subject dated "summer 1913" in a letter to
R. N. Ketterer, November 14, 1960.

39
Three Bathers (Drei Badende), ca. 1913
Oil on canvas. 79 x 59 in.
Lender: Anonymous loan
(Boston only)

References: R. Goldwater, *Primitivism in
Modern Painting,* 1938, (fig. 13); L. Buchheim,
Die Künstlergemeinschaft "Brücke," 1956,
(fig. 167); D. Gordon, *Kirchner,* 1968, no. 356.
Exhibitions: Frankfurt am Main, Galerie
Ludwig Schames, *Kirchner,* 1916, no. 10;
Cambridge, Mass., Busch-Reisinger Museum,
Kirchner, 1950–51; New York, Curt Valentin
Gallery, *Kirchner,* 1952, no. 7 (repr.); New
York, Curt Valentin Gallery, *Closing Ex-
hibition,* 1955, no. 52 (repr.).
A drawing in crayon is reproduced in
W. Grohmann, *Zeichnungen von Ernst
Ludwig Kirchner,* 1925, (fig. 51); lithograph
(Dube 237).

40
Berlin Street Scene
(Berliner Strassenszene), ca. 1913
Oil on canvas. 47⁵/₈ x 37¹/₂ in.
Signed, lower right: *E. L. Kirchner;* lower left
(pencil): *E. L. Kirchner*
Collections: Alfred Hess, Erfurt; Dr. Carl
Hagemann, Frankfurt am Main
Lender: Anonymous loan

References: L. Buchheim, *Die Künstlergemeinschaft Brücke,* 1956, (fig. 175);
K. Gerold, *Deutsche Malerei unserer Zeit,*
1956, (fig. 36); W. Grohmann, *E. L. Kirchner,*
1961, (repr. p. 45, color); D. Gordon, *Kirchner,*
1968, no. 363 (pl. XIII, color).
Exhibitions: Munich, Neue Staatsgalerie,
*Deutsche Malerei in den letzten fünfzig
Jahren,* 1924, no. 93 (repr.); Zürich, Kunsthaus, *Kirchner,* 1952, no. 34; Lucerne, Kunstmuseum, *Deutsche Kunst,* 1953, no. 45;
Essen, Museum Folkwang, *Brücke, 1905–
1913,* 1958, no. 90 (repr., color); Frankfurt am
Main, Kunstverein, *Moderne Malerei im
Frankfurter Privatbesitz,* 1963; Kassel,
Museum Fridericianum, *Documenta III,* 1964,
no. 2 (repr.); London, Tate Gallery, *Painters
of the "Brücke,"* 1964, no. 79; Basel, Kunsthalle, *E. L. Kirchner und Rot-Blau,* 1967,
no. 41 (repr.).
There is an etching of the same subject,
reversed (Dube 183).

41
Street, Berlin (Strasse, Berlin), ca. 1913
Color plate: p. 23
Oil on canvas. 47¹/₂ x 35⁷/₈ in.
Signed, lower right: *E. L. Kirchner*
Collection: Nationalgalerie, Berlin
Lender: The Museum of Modern Art,
New York

References: *Kunst und Künstler,* XVIII, no. 5,
1920, p. 229; Nationalgalerie, Berlin, *Ver-
zeichnis der Gemälde und Bildwerke,* 1921,
p. 61; 1923, p. 47; 1926, pp. 52, 58; The
Museum of Modern Art, New York, *Painting
and Sculpture in the Museum of Modern Art,*
1942, no. 317 (repr. p. 48); 1948, no. 371 (repr.
p. 79); B. Myers, "Ernst Ludwig Kirchner and
'Die Brücke,'" *Magazine of Art,* XLV, no. 1,
1952, (repr. p. 26); P. Selz, *German Expressionist Painting,* 1957, pp. 139–40, 285
(fig. 50); *New York Times,* Sept. 29, 1957,
(repr. p. 25); W. Grohmann, *E. L. Kirchner,*
1961, (repr. p. 117); F. Roh, *"Entartete" Kunst;
Kunstbarberei im dritten Reich,* 1961, p. 132;
D. Gordon, *Kirchner,* 1968, no. 364 (pl. 55).
Exhibitions: Berlin, Paul Cassirer, *Kirchner,*
1926, no. 21; New York, The Museum of
Modern Art, *German Painting and Sculpture,*
1931, no. 38 (repr.); Boston, Institute of
Modern Art, *Contemporary German Art,* 1939,
no. 25 (repr.); New York, The Museum of
Modern Art, *Art in our Time,* 1939, no. 126
(repr.); Cambridge, Mass., Busch-Reisinger
Museum, *Kirchner,* 1950–51; New York, The
Museum of Modern Art and St. Louis, City
Art Museum, *German Art of the Twentieth
Century,* 1957–58, no. 72 (repr., color);
Düsseldorf, Kunsthalle, *Kirchner,* 1960,
no. 51 (repr.); Columbus, Ohio, Gallery of
Fine Arts, *German Expressionism,* 1961,
no. 33 (repr.); Munich, Haus der Kunst,
Entartete Kunst; Bildersturm vor 25 Jahren,
1962, no. 65 (repr., color).

42
Two Women on the Street
(Zwei Frauen auf der Strasse), ca. 1914
Oil on canvas. 47¼ x 36¼ in.
Signed, left: *E. L. Kirchner*
Collections: Rosi Fischer, Frankfurt am Main;
Paul Westheim, Berlin
Lender: Mrs. Mariana Frenk-Westheim,
Mexico City

References: *Kunst und Künstler,* XVIII, no. 5,
1920, (repr. p. 227); D. Gordon, *Kirchner,*
1968, no. 369 (pl. 58).
Exhibition: Berlin, Nationalgalerie, *Neuere
deutsche Kunst aus Berliner Privatbesitz,*
1928, no. 59.
A pastel of the same subject is in the exhibition (Cat. no. 86), collection of Dr. and
Mrs. Ernst Fischer, Albany.

43
Self-Portrait as a Soldier
(Selbstbildnis als Soldat), ca. 1915
Oil on canvas. 27¼ x 24 in.
Signed, lower right: *E. L. Kirchner*
Collections: Städtische Galerie, Dresden;
Städelsches Kunstinstitut, Frankfurt am Main;
Kurt Feldhäusser, Berlin
Lender: Allen Memorial Art Museum,
Oberlin College

References: *Jahrbuch der jungen Kunst,*
1923, p. 363; *Allen Memorial Art Museum
Bulletin,* XI, no. 2, 1954, (fig. 70); B. Myers,
The German Expressionists, 1957, p. 132 (fig.
26); P. Selz, *German Expressionist Painting,*
1957, pp. 299–300 (fig. 139); P. Selz, "Kirchner's Self-Portrait as a Soldier in Relation to
Earlier Self-Portraits," *Allen Memorial Art
Museum Bulletin,* XIV, no. 3, 1957, pp. 91–97
(repr. p. 90); W. Grohmann, *E. L. Kirchner,*
1958, p. 68; M. Gasser, *Self-Portraits from the
Fifteenth Century to the Present Day,* 1961,
(repr. p. 265, color); F. Roh, *"Entartete"
Kunst; Kunstbarbarei im dritten Reich,* 1962,
p. 185; *Life,* November 29, 1963, (repr. p. 96,
color); D. Gordon, *Kirchner,* 1968, no. 435
(pl. 66).
Exhibitions: Munich, Bibliotheksbau des
deutschen Museums, *Der Bolshewismus,*
1936; Munich, Haus der Kunst, *Entartete
Kunst; Bildersturm vor 25 Jahren,* 1937; New
York, Curt Valentin Gallery, *Kirchner,* 1952,
no. 8; Cincinnati, Modern Art Association, *In
the Flat and Round,* 1952; New York, Knoed-
ler Galleries, *Paintings and Drawings from
Five Centuries,* 1954, no. 70 (repr.); Cambridge, Mass., Busch-Reisinger Museum,
War and Aftermath, 1957; Raleigh, North
Carolina Museum of Art, *Kirchner,* 1958,
no. 23 (repr.); Toledo, Museum of Art, *What
is Modern Art?,* 1960; Kansas City, Nelson
Gallery and Atkins Museum, *The Logic of
Modern Art,* 1961, no. 9; London, County
Council, *An American University Collection*
(Allen Memorial Art Museum), 1962, no. 26
(repr.); The Minneapolis Institute of Arts,
*Treasures from the Allen Memorial Art
Museum,* 1966.

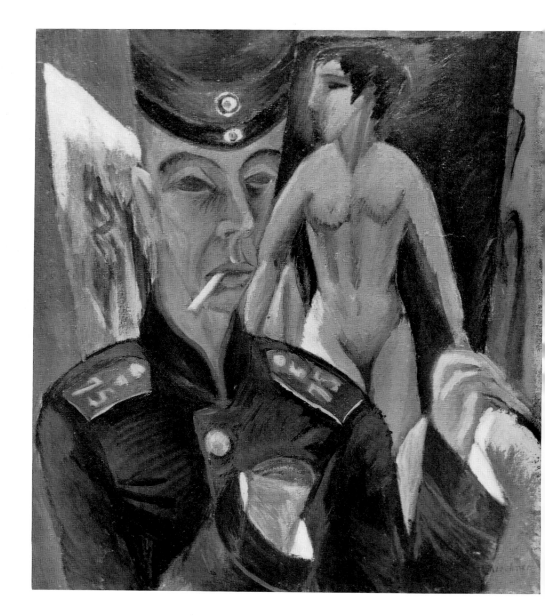

44
Brandenburg Gate, Berlin
(Brandenburger Tor, Berlin), ca. 1915
Oil on canvas. 20 x 27^1/$_2$ in.
Signed, lower right: *E. L. Kirchner*
Collection: Dr. Hans Koch, Randegg,
Germany
Lender: David Rockefeller, New York

References: *Kunstblatt*, VII, no. 3, 1923,
(repr. p. 76); D. Gordon, *Kirchner,* 1968, no.
437 (pl. 68).
Exhibitions: Frankfurt am Main, Galerie
Ludwig Schames, *Kirchner,* 1919, no. 10;
Bern, Kunsthalle, *Paula Modersohn und die
Maler der "Brücke,"* 1948, no. 63 (pl. 50,
color).

45

Gräf's Garden in Jena (Garten Gräf in Jena),
ca. 1916
Oil on canvas. 24¹/₂ x 20¹/₂ in.
Signed, upper right: *E. L. Kirchner*
Collection: Dr. Frederic Bauer, Davos
Lender: Kurt H. Grunebaum, Harrison,
New York

Reference: D. Gordon, *Kirchner*, 1968, no.
446 (pl. 69).
Exhibitions: Nuremberg, Munich, Freiburg,
Mannheim, Berlin, *Sammlung Dr. F. Bauer,
Davos,* 1952–53, no. 12 (repr.); Düsseldorf,
Galerie Wilhelm Grosshennig, *Kirchner,*
1954, no. 4; Columbus, Ohio, Gallery of Fine
Arts, *German Expressionism,* 1961, no. 35.

46

Königstein Train Station
(Bahnhof Königstein), 1917
Oil on canvas. 37 x 37 in.
Signed and dated, lower right:
E. L. Kirchner 17
Collections: Museum Folkwang, Essen; Kurt
Feldhäusser, Berlin
Lender: Dr. Max M. Stern, New York

References: Museum Folkwang, Essen,
Moderne Kunst, 1929, no. 184; P. Rave, *Kunst-
diktatur im dritten Reich,* 1949, (repr. p. 57);
F. Roh, *"Entartete" Kunst; Kunstbarbarei im
dritten Reich,* 1962, p. 160; A. Vellinghausen,
Anspielungen, 1962, p. 216 (repr. p. 217);
D. Gordon, *Kirchner,* 1968, no. 476 (pl. 74).
Exhibitions: Munich, Haus der Kunst, *Ent-
artete Kunst,* 1937; Düsseldorf, Kunsthalle,
Kirchner, 1960, no. 63 (repr.).

47

The Visit, Mrs. Binswanger
(Der Besuch, Frau Binswanger), 1917
Oil on canvas. 35 x 24 in.
Signed and dated, lower right:
E L Kirchner 17
Collection: Käthe Bernard-Robinson, Berlin
Lender: Anonymous loan

Reference: D. Gordon, *Kirchner,* 1968, no. 497
(pl. 77).
Exhibitions: Berlin, Nationalgalerie, *Neuere
deutsche Kunst aus Berliner Privatbesitz,*
1928, no. 66; Raleigh, North Carolina Museum
of Art, *Kirchner,* 1958, no. 24 (repr.).
There is a woodcut of the same subject,
reversed (Dube 315).

48

View of the Church in Monstein
(Blick auf die Kirche in Monstein),
ca. 1917–18
Oil on canvas. 30³/₄ x 21⁷/₈ in.
Signed, lower left: *E. L. Kirchner*
Lender: Hessisches Landesmuseum,
Darmstadt

Reference: D. Gordon, *Kirchner,* 1968, no. 505
(pl. XVII, color).
Exhibition: Basel, Kunsthalle, *E. L. Kirchner
und Rot-Blau,* 1967, no. 56.
There is an etching with drypoint of the same
subject, reversed (Dube 241).

49

Winter Moon Landscape
(Wintermondnacht), 1919
Color pl. p. 27
Oil on canvas. 47¹/₂ x 47¹/₂ in.
Signed, lower right: *E. L. Kirchner*
Collection: Kaiser-Friedrich-Museum,
Magdeburg
Lender: The Detroit Institute of Arts (Gift of
Curt Valentin on the 60th Birthday of
Dr. W. R. Valentiner)

References: A. Dressler, *Deutsche Kunst und
Entartete Kunst,* 1938, (repr. p. 70); W. Groh-
mann, *E. L. Kirchner,* 1958, p. 78 (repr. p. 121);
D. Gordon, *Kirchner,* 1968, no. 558 (pl. XIX,
color).
Exhibitions: Darmstadt, Mathildenhöhe,
Deutscher Expressionismus, 1920, no. 343;
Frankfurt am Main, Galerie Ludwig Schames,
Schweizer Arbeit von E. L. Kirchner, 1922,
no. 15; Munich, Haus der Kunst, *Entartete
Kunst,* 1937; San Francisco, Golden Gate
International Exposition, 1939, no. 24; Spring-
field, Mass., Museum of Fine Arts, *Modern
German Art,* 1939, no. 33, Baltimore, Museum
of Art, *Themes and Variations in Painting
and Sculpture,* 1948, no. 110; Minneapolis,
University of Minnesota, *German Expres-
sionism,* 1951, no. 47; Oberlin, Ohio, Allen
Memorial Art Museum, *Die Brücke,* 1951;
Raleigh, North Carolina Museum of Art,
Kirchner, 1958, no. 26 (repr.); Düsseldorf,
Kunsthalle, *Kirchner,* 1960, no. 68 (repr.).
There is a color woodcut of the same
subject, reversed (Dube 390) in this ex-
hibition, Cat. no. 134.

50
Seehorn, ca. 1919
Oil on cloth. 37³/₄ x 32¹/₈ in.
Collection: Kirchner Estate
Lender: Frau Hanna Bekker vom Rath,
Hofheim am Taunus

Reference: D. Gordon, *Kirchner,* 1968,
no. 565.
Exhibitions: Frankfurt am Main, Galerie
Ludwig Schames, *Kirchner,* 1925, no. 13;
St. Gallen, Kunstmuseum, *Kirchner,* 1950,
no. 34; Salonika, Athens, Beirut, *Deutsche
Kunst von 1910 bis zur Gegenwart,* 1962–63,
no. 49 (repr.).

51
Alp Hut, Red Alp House
(Alphütte, Rotes Alphaus), 1919
Oil on canvas. 47¹/₂ x 59¹/₂ in.
Signed, lower right: *E. L. Kirchner*
Collection: Kirchner Estate
Lender: Staatliche Kunsthalle, Karlsruhe

References: J. Roethel, *Moderne deutsche
Malerei,* 1957, (repr. p. 22, color); J. Lauts,
*Meisterwerke der Staatlichen Kunsthalle
Karlsruhe,* 1957, p. 48, no. 112 (pl. 118);
E. Langni, *50 Jahre moderne Kunst,* 1959,
p. 309, no. 148 (repr. p. 163); L. Grote, *Euro-
päische Malerei in deutschen Galerien;
Meister des 20. Jahrhunderts,* 1964, (fig. 2);
*Jahrbuch der Staatlichen Kunstsammlungen
in Baden-Württemberg,* I, 1964, p. 14, no. 6;
Staatliche Kunsthalle, Karlsruhe, *Deutsche
Meister 1880–1930 aus der Staatlichen Kunst-
halle,* 1965, no. 13 (repr.); D. Gordon, *Kirch-
ner,* 1968, no. 600 (pl. 81).
Exhibitions: Frankfurt am Main, Galerie
Ludwig Schames, *Schweizer Arbeit von
E. L. Kirchner,* 1922, no. 20; Bern, Kunsthalle,
Kirchner, 1933, no. 27; Hamburg, Hannover,
Bremen, Wuppertal-Elberfeld, *Kirchner,
Werke aus dem Nachlass,* 1950–51, no. 16;
Zürich, Kunsthaus, *Kirchner,* 1952, no. 45;
Chur, Kunsthaus, *Kirchner, Gemälde und
Graphik aus der Davoser Zeit,* 1953, no. 2;
Karlsruhe, Staatliche Kunsthalle, *Kunst
unserer Zeit,* 1955, no. 46; Kassel, Museum
Fridericianum, *Documenta I; Kunst des
20. Jahrhunderts,* 1955, no. 266; Brussels,
Exposition Universelle, *50 ans d'art moderne,*
1958, no. 149 (pl. 99).

52

Girl in South Wind

(Mädchen im Föhn), ca. 1919–20
Oil on canvas. 31^1/$_2$ x 25^5/$_8$ in.
Signed, lower left: *E. L. Kirchner*
Lender: Dr. Carlo Bosshart, Riehen,
Switzerland

Reference: D. Gordon, *Kirchner,* 1968, no. 620
(pl. 83).
Exhibitions: Bern, Kunsthalle, *Kirchner,* 1933,
no. 35; Basel, Kunsthalle, *Kirchner,* 1937,
no. 233.

53

Self-Portrait with a Cat

(Selbstporträt mit Katze), 1920
Oil on canvas. 47^1/$_4$ x 33^1/$_2$ in.
Signed, lower left: *E. L. Kirchner*
Collections: Museum Folkwang, Essen; Kurt
Feldhäusser, Berlin
Lender: Busch-Reisinger Museum, Harvard
University
(Boston only)

References: W. Grohmann, *Das Werk Ernst
Ludwig Kirchners,* 1926, (fig. 62); *Museum
der Gegenwart,* III, 1932/33, (fig. 19); B. Myers,
"Ernst Ludwig Kirchner and *Die Brücke,*"
Magazine of Art, XLV, no. 1, 1952, pp. 20–26
(repr. p. 26); C. Kuhn and J. Rosenberg,
*German Expressionism and Abstract Art;
The Harvard Collections,* 1957, p. 51 (fig. 7);
B. Myers, *The German Expressionists,* 1957,
p. 132; W. Grohmann, *E. L. Kirchner,* 1961,
(repr. p. 141); F. Roh, *"Entartete" Kunst;
Kunstbarbarei im dritten Reich,* 1962, p. 163;
L. Grisebach, *Maler des Expressionismus in
Briefwechsel mit Eberhard Grisebach,* 1962,
(repr. p. 112 bis); P. Vogt, *Das Museum
Folkwang Essen,* 1965, (fig. 45); *L'Arte
Moderna,* III, no. 2, 1967, p. 143; D. Gordon,
Kirchner, 1968, no. 621 (pl. 84).
Exhibitions: Frankfurt am Main, Galerie
Ludwig Schames, *Schweizer Arbeit von
E. L. Kirchner,* 1922, no. 27 (repr.); Cam-
bridge, Mass., Busch-Reisinger Museum,
Kirchner, 1950–51; Minneapolis, University
of Minnesota, *German Expressionism,* 1951,
no. 49; Boston, Museum of Fine Arts,
European Masters of Our Time, 1957, no. 50
(fig. 78); Raleigh, North Carolina Museum of
Art, *Kirchner, 1958,* no. 29 (repr.); Düsseldorf,
Kunsthalle, *Kirchner,* 1960, no. 66 (repr.);
Kassel, Museum Fridericianum, *Documenta
III,* 1964, no. 4 (repr.).
There is a woodcut of the same subject,
reversed (Dube 428).

54

The Blue Tree, Mountain Forest
(Der blaue Baum, Bergwald), 1920
Oil on canvas. 47¹/₄ x 47¹/₄ in.
Collection: Nationalgalerie (Kronprinzen-
palais), Berlin
Lender: Dr. Rüdiger Graf von der Goltz,
Düsseldorf

References: W. Grohmann, *Das Werk Ernst
Ludwig Kirchners*, 1926, (fig. 70); D. Gordon,
Kirchner, 1968, no. 651 (pl. 87).
Exhibition: Düsseldorf, Kunsthalle, *Kirchner*,
1960, no. 72 (repr., color).
Kirchner includes a sketch in ink for this
painting in a letter to Nele van de Velde,
February 20, 1921. He first mentions the
painting in progress and records the final
completion in letters to Henry van de Velde,
October 27, 1920, and November 5, 1922,
respectively.

55

Woman and Girl, Mother and Daughter
(Frau und Mädchen, Mutter und Mädchen),
1922–23
Oil on canvas. 66¹/₈ x 46⁷/₈ in.
Signed and dated, upper right: *E. L. Kirch-
ner 23*
Collections: Staatliche Gemäldegalerie,
Dresden; Frau Maria Möller-Garny, Cologne
Lender: Seattle Art Museum

References: *Europa Almanach*, 1925, (repr.
p. 73); *Cicerone*, XX, p. 166; *100 Jahre
Sächsischer Kunstverein, Jubiläums-
Festschrift*, II, 1928, (repr. p. 27); Staatliche
Gemäldegalerie, Dresden, *Katalog Moderne
Galerie*, 1930, p. 99; F. Roh, *"Entartete"
Kunst; Kunstbarbarei im dritten Reich*, 1962,
p. 150; D. Gordon, *Kirchner*, 1968, no. 692
(pl. 89).
Exhibitions: Winterthur, Kunstverein, *Kirch-
ner*, 1924, no. 31; Frankfurt am Main, Galerie
Ludwig Schames, *Kirchner*, 1925, no. 38;
Lucerne, Kunstmuseum, *Deutsche Kunst*,
1953, no. 52; Düsseldorf, Kunsthalle,
Kirchner, 1960, no. 78 (repr.).

56

The Flute Player (Der Flötenspieler), 1922–23
Oil on canvas. 46¹/₂ x 35 in.
Signed, upper left: *E. L. Kirchner*
Collection: Dr. Hans Staub-Oetiker, Zürich
Lender: Prof. Hans Staub, Zürich

Reference: D. Gordon, *Kirchner,* 1968,
no. 709.
There is an etching with drypoint of the
same subject, reversed (Dube 305). Prof.
Hans Staub, the present owner, is the subject
of the painting, for which he posed in "1922
or 1923," shortly before Kirchner's move
from the Langematte house.

57

Davos in the Snow (Davos im Schnee), 1923
Oil on canvas. 47⁵/₈ x 59¹/₈ in.
Signed, lower right: *E L Kirchner*
Collection: Georg Reinhart, Winterthur
Lender: Oeffentliche Kunstsammlung, Basel
(Gift of Georg Reinhart)

References: W. Grohmann, *Das Werk Ernst
Ludwig Kirchners,* 1926, (fig. 79); *Werk,*
XXXV, no. 1, 1948, p. 22; *Kunstwerk,* 1952,
(repr. p. 27, color); W. Grohmann,
E. L. Kirchner, 1961, (repr. p. 149); D. Gordon,
Kirchner, 1968, no. 716 (pl. 90).
Exhibitions: Winterthur, Kunstverein,
Kirchner, 1924, no. 29; Zürich, Kunsthaus,
Kirchner, 1952, no. 53 (repr.).

8

Modern Bohemia

(Bohême moderne), ca. 1924
Oil on canvas. 49¼ x 65⅛ in.
Signed, lower left: *E. L. Kirchner*
Collection: Museum Folkwang, Essen
Lender: The Minneapolis Institute of Arts
(Bequest of Curt Valentin)

References: W. Grohmann, *Das Werk Ernst
Ludwig Kirchners,* 1926, (fig. 96); C. Kessler,
"Sun Worship and Anxiety; Nature,
Nakedness and Nihilism in German Expressionist Painting," *Magazine of Art,* XLV, no. 7,
1952, pp. 304–12, (repr. p. 311); The Minne-
polis Institute of Arts, *Bulletin,* 1956, XLV,
no. 2, pp. 17–19 (repr.); W. Haftmann, *Malerei
in 20. Jahrhundert,* 1962, II, (repr. p. 314);
The Nelson Gallery of Art, Kansas City,
Gallery News, 1955, p. 1; F. Roh, *"Entartete"
Kunst; Kunstbarbarei im dritten Reich,* 1962,
p. 163; *European Paintings in the Minneap-
lis Institute of Arts,* 1963, p. 73; D. Gordon,
Kirchner, 1968, no. 767 (pl. XXII, color).

Exhibitions: Düsseldorf, *Jubiläumsausstel-
ung,* 1925, no. 1165; New York, The Museum
of Modern Art, *German Painting and Sculp-
ure,* 1931, no. 41 (repr.); Cambridge, Mass.,
Busch-Reisinger Museum, *Kirchner,* 1950–51;
New York, Curt Valentin Gallery, *Kirchner,*
1952, no. 14 (repr.); Kansas City, The Nelson
Gallery of Art, *Modern Masterpiece of the
Month,* March, 1955; New York, Fine Arts
Associates, *Collectors: Their Faces,* 1958.
There is a drawing in pen and ink with
watercolor of the same subject in the
Städelsches Kunstinstitut, Frankfurt; color
woodcut, reversed (Dube 525) in this ex-
hibition, Cat. no. 140.

9

Landscape in Spring, Sertig

(Frühlingslandschaft, Sertig), ca. 1924–25
Oil on canvas. 39⅜ x 46⅞ in.
Signed, upper left: *E. L. Kirchner*
Collection: Kirchner Estate
Lender: Mrs. William A. Bernoudy, St. Louis
(Boston only)

References: *Davoser Revue,* XIII, June 9,
1938, p. 190; D. Gordon, *Kirchner,* 1968,
no. 795 (pl. 92).

60
House in Autumn, The Painter's House
(Haus im Herbst, Haus des Malers), 1925
Oil on canvas. 47¹/₄ x 35¹/₂ in.
Signed (scratched), lower right: *E. L. Kirchner;* (scratched), lower left: *K*
Collection: Kirchner Estate
Lender: Walter Haller, Biberach/Riss

Reference: D. Gordon, *Kirchner,* 1968, no. 817 (pl. 93).
Kirchner mentions the start of this painting and the painting in progress in his diary, pp. 172–73, October 6 and 15, 1925.

61
White House in Sertigtal
(Weisses Haus im Sertigtal), ca. 1926
Oil on canvas. 36 x 46 in.
Collection: Kirchner Estate
Lender: Anonymous loan

Reference: D. Gordon, *Kirchner,* 1968, no. 845 (pl. 94).
Exhibition: New York, Fine Arts Associates, *Kirchner,* 1957, no. 20.

62

The Bridge at Wiesen

(Die Brücke bei Wiesen), ca. 1926
Oil on canvas. 46$^7/_8$ x 46$^1/_4$ in.
Signed, lower right: *E. L. Kirchner*
Lender: Landschaft Davos, Switzerland
(Municipality of Davos)

References: *Davoser Blätter*, LXVII, no. 21,
July 8, 1938, (repr. p. 6); W. Kern, *Graubünden in der Malerei*, 1941, (fig. 1);
D. Gordon, *Kirchner*, 1968, no. 844
(p. XXIII, color).

63

View of Dresden, Schlossplatz

(Blick auf Dresden, Schlossplatz), ca. 1926
Oil on canvas. 47 x 58$^3/_4$ in.
Signed, lower left: *E. L. Kirchner*
Collection: Kirchner Estate
Lender: Mr. and Mrs. John Cowles,
Minneapolis

References: *College Art Journal*, XIX, no. 1,
1959, (repr. p. 89); D. Gordon, *Kirchner*, 1968,
no. 856.
Exhibitions: Bern, Kunsthalle, *Kirchner*,
1933, no. 73; The Detroit Institute of Arts,
Kirchner, 1937; New York, Buchholz Gallery-
Curt Valentin, *Kirchner*, 1937, no. 6;
Cambridge, Mass., Busch-Reisinger
Museum, *Kirchner*, 1950–51; New York, Curt
Valentin Gallery, 1951, no. 27 (repr.);
Northampton, Mass., Smith College Museum
of Art, *Paintings from Smith Alumnae Col-
lections*, 1959, no. 27 (repr. facing p. 66).

64

Mountain Landscape from Clavadel
(Berglandschaft von Clavadel), 1927
Oil on canvas. 53 x 79 in.
Signed, lower right: *E L Kirchner;*
(scratched) upper right: *K*
Collection: Kirchner Estate
Lender: Museum of Fine Arts, Boston
(Arthur Gordon Tompkins Residuary Fund)

Reference: D. Gordon, *Kirchner,* 1968,
no. 891 (pl. 98).
Exhibitions: Bern, Kunsthalle, *Kirchner,*
1933, no. 71 (repr.); Davos, Kunstgesellschaft, Schulhaus, Davos-Platz, *Graubünden
in der Malerei und Gedächtnisausstellung
E. L. Kirchner,* 1938, no. 127; St. Gallen,
Kunstmuseum, *Kirchner,* 1950, no. 38; Chur,
Kunsthaus, *Kirchner: Gemälde und Graphik
aus der Davoser Zeit,* 1953, no. 15; Raleigh,
North Carolina Museum of Art, *Kirchner,*
1958, no. 36 (repr.); Pasadena Art Museum,
German Expressionism, 1961, no. 46.
The figures are Hans Schiess, Lise Gujer
and Erna Kirchner, according to Miss Gujer
in an interview, May, 1965. Kirchner mentions
Schiess' visit from June through September,
1927, in his diary, p. 363, September, 1927.

65

Mountains with Skiers
(Schneeberge mit Skiläufern), 1928
Oil on canvas. 35$^1/_2$ x 47$^1/_4$ in.
Signed, center right: *E. L. Kirchner 28*
Collection: Kirchner Estate
Lender: Ernesto Blohm, Caracas

References: *Kunstwerk,* V, no. 3, 1951,
(repr. p. 20); D. Gordon, *Kirchner,* 1968,
no. 928.
Exhibitions: Bern, Kunsthalle, *Kirchner,*
1933, no. 81; Hamburg, Hannover, Bremen,
Wuppertal-Elberfeld, *Kirchner, Werke aus
dem Nachlass,* 1950–51, no. 29 (repr.).

66
Meadow Flowers and Cat
(Wiesenblumen und Katze), ca. 1931
Oil on canvas. 53$^{1}/_{4}$ x 35$^{1}/_{2}$ in.
Signed, lower right: *E. L. Kirchner*
Collection: Kirchner Estate
Lender: Ernesto Blohm, Caracas

Reference: D. Gordon, *Kirchner,* 1968,
no. 955 (pl. 105).
Exhibition: Bern, Kunsthalle, *Kirchner,*
1933, no. 102.

99

67

Hockey Players (Eishockeyspieler), 1934
Oil on canvas. 31¹/₂ x 27¹/₂ in.
Signed and dated, lower right: *E. L. Kirch-*
ner 34
Collections: Wilhelm R. Valentiner, Raleigh;
The Cleveland Museum of Art
Lender: Marlborough-Gerson Gallery, Inc.,
New York

Reference: D. Gordon, *Kirchner,* 1968,
no. 976 (pl. 108).
Exhibitions: The Detroit Institute of Arts,
Kirchner, 1937; New York, Buchholz Gallery-
Curt Valentin, *Kirchner,* 1937, no. 12; Ann
Arbor, University of Michigan Museum of
Art, *Sport and Circus,* 1950; Raleigh, North
Carolina Museum of Art, *Kirchner,* 1958,
no. 40 (repr.).
There is a watercolor of the same subject
in the collection of William Zeckendorf,
New York.

68

Sertig Path (Sertigweg), ca. 1937
Oil on canvas. 47³/₈ x 39³/₄ in.
Signed (scratched), upper left: *E. L. Kirchner;*
(scratched), lower left: *ELK*
Collections: Dr. Frederic Bauer, Davos;
Mrs. Heinz Schultz, Great Neck, New York
Lenders: Mr. and Mrs. Stephen Adler, Hollis-
wood, New York

Reference: D. Gordon, *Kirchner,* 1968,
no. 1015 (pl. XXVII, color).
Exhibitions: Basel, Kunsthalle, *Kirchner,*
1937, no. 258; Nuremberg, Munich, Freiburg,
Mannheim, Berlin, *Sammlung Dr. F. Bauer,*
Davos, 1952, no. 27 (repr.).

69
Forest Interior (Waldinneres), 1937
Oil on canvas. 69⅞ x 53⅜ in.
Signed, lower right: *E. L. Kirchner*
Collection: Dr. Stöckli, Davos
Lender: Anonymous loan

References: *Davoser Revue*, XIII, June 9,
1938, p. 191; D. Gordon, *Kirchner*, 1968,
no. 1017 (pl. XXVIII, color).
Exhibitions: Davos, Kunstgesellschaft,
Schulhaus, Davos-Platz, *Graubunden in der
Malerei und Gedächtnisausstellung E. L.
Kirchner*, 1938, no. 118; Zürich, Kunsthaus,
Kirchner, 1952, no. 70; Stuttgart, Württembergischer Kunstverein, *Kirchner*, 1956,
no. 31.
There is a sketch in ink of this painting in
a letter to Dr. Carl Hagemann, September,
1937. Kirchner mentions the painting in progress in letters to Dr. Hagemann, August 28
and September, 1937.

70
Junkerboden in the Snow
(Junkerboden im Schnee), ca. 1936–38
Oil on canvas. 39 x 47¼ in.
Signed (scratched), upper right: *E. L.
Kirchner*
Collections: Kirchner Estate; Alex Voemel,
Düsseldorf
Lender: Dr. Max M. Stern, New York

Reference: D. Gordon, *Kirchner*, 1968,
no. 1018.
Exhibitions: New York, Fine Arts Associates,
Kirchner, 1957, no. 13; New York, Marlborough-Gerson Gallery, *A Tribute to Curt
Valentin*, 1963, no. 255, p. 137 (repr.); London,
Marlborough Fine Art Ltd., *Recent Acquisitions*, 1967, no. 11 (repr.); New York, Marlborough-Gerson Gallery, *International Expressionism, Part I*, 1968, no. 24 (repr.).

71

Herd of Sheep (Schafherde), 1938
Oil on canvas. 30¹/₂ x 47¹/₄ in.
Signed, lower left: *E. L. Kirchner;*
(scratched), lower right: *K;* (scratched),
upper right: *ELK*
Collections: Kirchner Estate; Arthur
L. Caplan, Los Angeles; University of
California Art Galleries, Los Angeles
Lender: Felix Landau Gallery, Los Angeles

Reference: D. Gordon, Kirchner, 1968,
no. 1024 (pl. 113).
Exhibitions: Cambridge, Mass., Busch-
Reisinger Museum, *Kirchner,* 1950–51;
New York, Curt Valentin Gallery, *Kirchner,*
1952, no. 25 (repr.); Los Angeles, Paul
Kantor Gallery, *Kirchner,* 1957, no. 12 (repr.);
Raleigh, North Carolina Museum of Art,
Kirchner, 1958, no. 43 (repr.); Düsseldorf,
Kunsthalle, *Kirchner,* 1960, no. 105 (repr.).
The painting was found on Kirchner's easel
after his death, according to W. R. Valentiner
in *E. L. Kirchner,* Raleigh, 1958 (exhibition
catalogue), p. 30. It is called "his last
picture" by Mrs. Erna Kirchner, in a letter
to Dr. Valentiner, June 15, 1938 (*ibid.,* p. 49).

72
Sketchbook, ca. 1906–11
Various media
Collection: Wilhelm R. Valentiner, Raleigh
Lender: Mrs. Brigitta Valentiner Bertoia,
Barto, Pennsylvania

Exhibition: Raleigh, North Carolina Museum
of Art, *Kirchner,* 1958, nos. 44 and 45 (repr.).

73
Reclining Nude on Sofa
(Liegender Rückenakt auf Sofa), 1907
Pencil and black chalk. $27\frac{1}{2}$ x 36 in.
Signed and dated, lower left center:
E. L. Kirchner 04
Collection: Private Collection, Stuttgart,
1965.
Lenders: Mr. and Mrs. D. Thomas Bergen,
London (On long-term loan to the Art
Institute of Chicago)

Exhibitions: London, Marlborough Fine Art.
Ltd., *Expressionism—Bauhaus—Dada,* 1966,
no. 21 (repr.); New York, Marlborough-
Gerson Gallery, *Modern Masters, Drawings
and Watercolors,* 1966; London, Marlborough
Fine Art. Ltd., *Drawings and Watercolours,*
1967, no. 27.

74
Emmy Frisch, 1908
(Verso: Two Nudes, colored crayon and
watercolor, 1910)
Gouache. $23\frac{5}{8}$ x $19\frac{5}{8}$ in.
Lender: Galerie Nierendorf, Berlin

75
Woman with Black Hat
(Dame mit schwarzem Hut), 1908
Watercolor. 18 x 13⁵/₈ in.
Lender: Mrs. Heinz Schultz, Great Neck,
New York

Nude (Akt), 1909
Brush and ink. 17⁵/₈ x 13¹/₂ in.
Lender: The Museum of Modern Art,
New York (Anonymous Gift)

77
Potholder District, Dresden
(Topflappenviertel, Dresden), 1909
Colored crayon. 13$^7/_{16}$ x 17$^7/_{16}$ in.
Lender: Galerie Nierendorf, Berlin

78
Boats on the Elbe (Elbzillen), 1909–10
Watercolor and pencil. 8$^1/_2$ x 11$^7/_{16}$ in.
Lender: Galerie Nierendorf, Berlin

79
Fränzi in an Interior (Fränzi), 1910
Gouache. 13$^3/_4$ x 17$^3/_4$ in.
Collection: Stroeher collection
Lenders: Mr. and Mrs. Hall James Peterson,
Minneapolis

0
Portrait of a Young Woman
(Damenporträt), ca. 1912
Pencil. 21 5/16 x 15 3/8 in.
Signed, lower right: *E L Kirchner*
Lender: The Art Institute of Chicago

Exhibition: New York (Guggenheim),
Minneapolis, Cambridge, Mass. (Fogg),
20th Century Master Drawings, 1963–64,
no. 53 (repr.).

1
Reclining Figure by the Rocks
(Liegende "An den Steinen"), 1912
Pen and ink. 17 1/4 x 22 7/8 in.
Signed and dated, lower right:
E. L. Kirchner 12
Lender: Dr. Rüdiger Graf von der Goltz,
Düsseldorf

Exhibition Düsseldorf, Kunsthalle, *Kirchner,*
1960, no. 42 (repr.).

82
Two Figures (Zwei Akte), ca. 1912
Watercolor and pencil. 21⁵/₈ x 15¹/₄ in. (Sight)
Signed, lower right: *E L Kirchner*
Collection: Galka E. Scheyer, Los Angeles
Lender: Pasadena Art Museum
(Galka Scheyer Collection)

83
Portrait of Dr. Döblin, 1913
Black and colored chalk. 16 x 14¹/₁₆ in.
Signed, center right: *E L Kirchner;* lower
right: *Dr. Döblin / E L Kirchner*
Lender: Städtische Galerie, Frankfurt am
Main

Reference: W. Grohmann, *Kirchner-Zeichnungen,* 1925, (pl. 46).
Exhibition: Düsseldorf, Kunsthalle, *Kirchner,*
1960, no. 58 (repr.).

Streetwalkers
(Kokotten auf der Strasse), 1913
Pen, pencil and wash. 18¹⁵/16 x 14⁵/8 in.
Signed and dated, lower right:
E. L. Kirchner 11
Lender: Dr. Rüdiger Graf von der Goltz,
Düsseldorf

Exhibition: Düsseldorf, Kunsthalle, *Kirchner,*
1960, no. 47 (repr.).

85
Street Scene, Berlin
(Strassenszene, Berlin), 1913
Colored crayon. 8 x 6³/16 in.
Lender: Galerie Nierendorf, Berlin

86
Streetwalkers (Zwei Kokotten), 1914
Pastel. 26¹/₂ x 20 in.
Lenders: Dr. and Mrs. Ernst Fischer, Albany

Reference: W. Grohmann, *Kirchner-Zeichnungen,* 1925, (pl. 52).
Exhibitions: Raleigh, North Carolina Museum of Art, *Kirchner,* 1958, no. 46 (repr.); Düsseldorf, Kunsthalle, *Kirchner,* 1960, no. 49 (repr.).
A preparatory study for *Two Women on the Street* lent by Mrs. Mariana Frenk-Westheim Cat. no. 42 in the exhibition.

87
Standing Nude in the Bathtub
(Stehender Akt in Badewanne), 1914
Colored crayon. 25 x 18 in.
Signed and dated, lower left:
E. L. Kirchner 14
Lender: Mrs. Ala Story, Santa Barbara

Reference: L. Buchheim, *Die Künstlergemeinschaft Brücke,* 1956, (pl. 207).
Exhibitions: Los Angeles, Paul Kantor Gallery, *Kirchner,* 1957, no. 17; Phoenix Art Museum, *The Collection of Margaret Mallory – Ala Story,* 1962; Santa Barbara Museum of Art and San Francisco, California Palace of the Legion of Honor, *Two Collections,* 1966.

48
Woman in Interior, Dressing
(Sich ankleidende Frau), ca. 1914
Oil, crayon, and pastel. 26¼ x 20⅜ in.
Signed, lower right (pencil): *E. L. Kirchner*
Lender: Achenbach Foundation for Graphic
Arts, California Palace of the Legion of
Honor, San Francisco

49
Sailor Saying Goodbye
(Matrose sich verabschiedend), 1914–15
Crayon, brush and ink. 16⅞ x 20 in.
Lender: The Museum of Modern Art, New
York (Gift of Mr. and Mrs. Eugene Victor
Thaw)

Exhibition: Raleigh, North Carolina Museum
of Art, *Kirchner,* 1958, no. 47 (repr.).

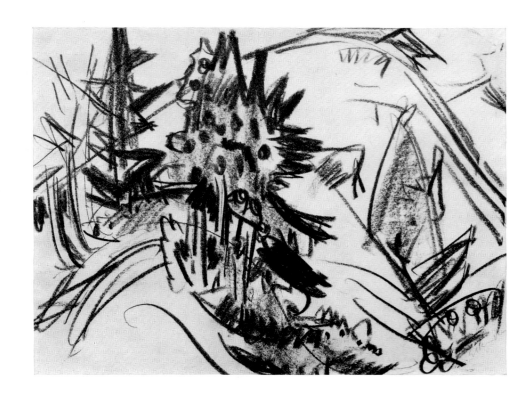

90
Cows (Kühe), 1918
Pen, pencil and wash. 15¹¹/₁₆ x 19⁷/₁₆ in.
Lender: Dr. Rüdiger Graf von der Goltz,
Düsseldorf

Exhibition: Düsseldorf, Kunsthalle, *Kirchner,*
1960, no. 74 (repr.).

91
Mountain Landscape
(Berglandschaft), ca. 1920
Black crayon on yellow paper. 11¹/₈ x 14⁵/₈ in.
Signed, lower right: *E L Kirchner*
Collection: Hans Klihm, Munich
Lenders: Mr. and Mrs. Perry T. Rathbone,
Cambridge, Massachusetts

Exhibitions: Cambridge, Mass., Fogg Art
Museum, 1958; Raleigh, North Carolina
Museum of Art, *Kirchner,* 1958, no. 50 (repr.).

92
Girls in a Forest (Mädchen im Walde), 1921
Watercolor. 18¹⁵/₁₆ x 15¹/₁₆ in.
Signed, lower left: *E. L. Kirchner*
Lender: Dr. Rüdiger Graf von der Goltz,
Düsseldorf

Reference: W. Grohmann, *Kirchner-Zeichnungen,* 1925, (pl. 89).
Exhibition: Düsseldorf, Kunsthalle, *Kirchner,*
1960, no. 126 (repr.).

93
Peasant Group out of Doors
(Bauern im Freien), ca. 1922
Watercolor. 14 x 19 in.
Lenders: Mr. and Mrs. S. J. Levin, St. Louis

Exhibition: Raleigh, North Carolina Museum of Art, *Kirchner,* 1958, no. 52 (repr.).

94
Portrait of Gustav Schiefler, 1923
Pen and ink. 17$^1/_8$ x 14$^3/_{16}$ in.
Collection: Kirchner Estate
Lender: The Art Institute of Chicago

Exhibition: Chicago, The Arts Club, *Drawings 1916/1966,* 1966, no. 49.

95
Wildboden Interior
(Wildboden, Interieur), ca. 1924
Pen and ink. 13$^1/_2$ x 20$^3/_8$ in.
Signed, lower right: *E L Kirchner*
Collection: Kirchner Estate
Lenders: Mr. and Mrs. D. Thomas Bergen, London (On long-term loan to the Art Institute of Chicago)

References: E. Wiese, "Zeichnungen von E. L. Kirchner," *Monatshefte für Bücherfreunde und Graphiksammler,* no. 2, 1925, (repr. p. 463); B. Myers, *The German Expressionists,* 1957, (repr. p. 129).
Exhibition: Minneapolis, Walker Art Center, *Third Collectors Exhibition,* 1962.

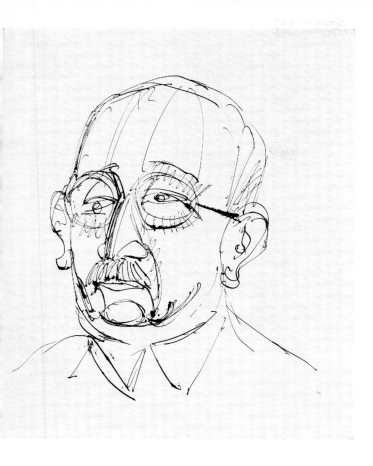

96
Landscape at Frauenkirch
(Landschaft, Frauenkirch), 1924–25
Watercolor. 16¼ x 19⅝ in.
Signed, lower right: *E. L. Kirchner*
Lenders: Mr. and Mrs. Perry T. Rathbone,
Cambridge, Massachusetts

Exhibitions: Minneapolis, University of
Minnesota, *German Expressionism,* 1951;
Indianapolis, Herron Museum of Art, 1951;
Raleigh, North Carolina Museum of Art,
Kirchner, 1958, no. 51 (repr.); Pasadena Art
Museum, *German Expressionism,* 1961.

97
Moonlit Night (Mondnacht), 1925
Watercolor. 13³/₁₆ x 18⁵/₁₆ in.
Signed and dated, lower right:
E. L. Kirchner 25
Lender: Dr. Rüdiger Graf von der Goltz,
Düsseldorf

Exhibition: Düsseldorf, Kunsthalle, *Kirchner,*
1960, no. 94 (repr.).

98
Alpine Village (Berglandschaft), ca. 1925–27
Watercolor. $7^3/_4$ x $13^1/_2$ in.
Signed, lower left: *E L Kirchner*
Lender: Mrs. Heinz Schultz, Great Neck,
New York

99
Ski Jumpers (Die Sprungschanzer), 1927
Watercolor. 12 x 10 in. (Sight)
Collection: Mr. and Mrs. S. J. Levin, St. Louis
Lender: Fine Arts Museum, George Peabody
College, Nashville, Tennessee

Exhibition: Raleigh, North Carolina Museum
of Art, *Kirchner,* 1958, no. 56 (repr.).

100
Interior of a Forest (Waldinneres), ca. 1930
Black and colored crayon. $16^5/_8$ x $19^7/_8$ in.
Collection: Kirchner Estate
Lender: Museum of Fine Arts, Boston
(Helen and Alice Colburn Fund)

101
Mountain Lake (Bergsee), 1930
Watercolor. 13³/₄ x 19⁷/₈ in.
Signed, lower left (pencil): *E L Kirchner*
Lender: The Detroit Institute of Arts (Gift of
John S. Newberry)

Exhibitions: Raleigh, North Carolina Museum
of Art, *Kirchner,* 1958, no. 54 (repr.); The
Detroit Institute of Arts, *The John S. Newberry Collection,* 1965, p. 49 (repr.); The
Detroit Institute of Arts, *German Expressionist Prints, Drawings and Water Colors: Die
Brücke,* 1967, no. 28 (repr.).

102
Twirling Dancer (Drehende Tänzerin), 1931
Watercolor. 20⁵/₁₆ x 14³/₁₆ in.
Signed, lower left: *E L Kirchner*
Collection: Dr. Carl Hagemann, Frankfurt am
Main
Lender: Städtische Galerie, Frankfurt am
Main

Exhibition: Düsseldorf, Kunsthalle, *Kirchner,*
1960, no. 112 (repr.).

129

103
Clockbelltower at Bern
(Zeitglockenturm Bern), 1933–34
Watercolor. 13^1/$_2$ x 20 in. (Sight)
Lender: Fogg Art Museum, Harvard University (Gift of Charles K. Lock)
(Seattle only)

104
Flowers in a Vase (Blumen), ca. 1935
Watercolor. 19^1/$_2$ x 13^1/$_2$ in. (Sight)
Signed, lower right: *E Kirchner*
Collection: Wilhelm R. Valentiner, Raleigh
Lender: North Carolina Museum of Art, Raleigh (Bequest of W. R. Valentiner)

Reference: *The Art Quarterly,* XXVI, no. 2, 1963, p. 275.
Exhibition: Raleigh, North Carolina Museum of Art, *Kirchner,* 1958, no. 58 (repr.).

105
Forest Clearing (Der Wald), 1935–37
Brush and watercolor on ink. $9^{11}/_{16}$ x $10^{1}/_{16}$ in.
Lender: Galerie Nierendorf, Berlin

Prints

This section is based on the recently published catalogue raisonné of Kirchner's prints by Drs. Annemarie and Wolf-Dieter Dube, *E. L. Kirchner — Das Graphische Werk,* I and II, Munich (Prestel-Verlag), 1967. Catalogue numbers from Dube and from the earlier catalogues of Kirchner's graphic work by Gustav Schiefler, I (1926) and II (1931) are included in each entry.

106
Title page for manifesto,
Künstlergruppe Brücke, 1906
Linoleum cut. 4^{15}/$_{16}$ x 2 in.
Not in Sch.; Dube 694.
Lender: The Museum of Modern Art,
New York (Gift of J. B. Neumann)

107
First page of manifesto,
Künstlergruppe Brücke, 1906
Linoleum cut. 6 x 2^{15}/$_{16}$ in.
Not in Sch.; Dube 696.
Lender: The Museum of Modern Art,
New York (Gift of J. B. Neumann)

108
Self-Portrait in Interior with Bed
(Selbstporträt in Kammer), 1907
Lithograph. 13¼ x 16 in.
Sch. 65; Dube 41.
Lender: Marion Koogler McNay Art Institute,
San Antonio

109
Women's Band (Damenkapelle), 1907–08
Etching, printed in green. 11 x 12⅛ in.
Sch. 10; Dube 32.
Lender: The Museum of Modern Art,
New York (Abby Aldrich Rockefeller Fund)

110
Self-Portrait with Pipe
(Selbstbildnis mit Pfeife), 1908
Drypoint. 8¹¹/₁₆ x 7⅞ in.
Sch. 50; Dube 27.
Lender: Wolfgang Budczies, Bremen

111
Embracing Couple (Liebesszene), 1908
Color lithograph. 14³/₄ x 12¹³/₁₆ in.
Sch. 75; Dube 73.
Lender: Wolfgang Budczies, Bremen

112
Street in Dresden
(Strassenleben in Dresden), 1908
Lithograph. 10⁵/₈ x 15¹/₈ in.
Sch. 38; Dube 55.
Lender: The Museum of Modern Art,
New York (Abby Aldrich Rockefeller Fund)

113
Actress Acknowledging Applause
(Beifallheischende Artistin), 1909
Color lithograph. 15$^{1}/_{8}$ x 12$^{7}/_{8}$ in.
Sch. 81; Dube 122.
Lender: Fogg Art Museum, Harvard
University

114
Dodo Reclining (Liegende Frau), 1909
Lithograph. 19$^{1}/_{2}$ x 23$^{3}/_{8}$ in.
Not in Sch.; Dube 105.
Lender: Fogg Art Museum, Harvard
University (Gift of Mrs. Heinz Schultz)

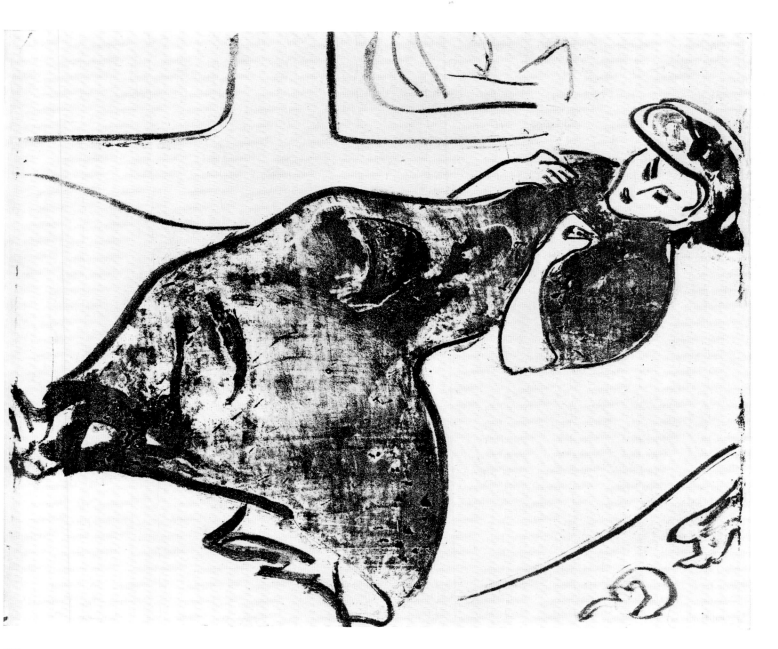

115
Girls on the Banks of the Elbe
(Mädchen am Elbkai), 1909
Color lithograph. 13 x 15³/₁₆ in.
Sch. 43; Dube 131.
Lender: Wolfgang Budczies, Bremen

116
Four Bathers
(Mit Schilf werfende Badende), 1910
Color woodcut. 7¹¹/₁₆ x 11³/₁₆ in.
Sch. 121; Dube 160.
Lenders: Mr. and Mrs. Perry T. Rathbone,
Cambridge, Massachusetts

117
Gerty with Mask and Wineglass
(Gerty mit Maske und Weinglas), 1910
Lithograph on yellow paper. 15¹/₈ x 12⁷/₈ in.
Sch. 78; Dube 143.
Lender: The Museum of Modern Art,
New York (Abby Aldrich Rockefeller Fund)

118
Two Dancers
(Russische Tänzerinnen mit Turban), 1911
Etching. 7¹⁵/₁₆ x 7³/₄ in.
Sch. 72; Dube 102.
Lenders: Dr. and Mrs. Ernst Fischer, Albany

119
Three Bathers by Rocks
(Drei Badende an Steinen), 1912
Color lithograph. 19$^{1}/_{2}$ x 23$^{1}/_{2}$ in.
Sch. 214; Dube 235.
Lender: Wolfgang Budczies, Bremen

120
Three Women in Cafe Garden
(Drei Frauen im Cafégarten), 1914
Lithograph. 19$^{7}/_{8}$ x 23$^{1}/_{2}$ in.
Sch. 248; Dube 243.
Lenders: Dr. and Mrs. Ernst Fischer, Albany

121
Women on Potsdamer Platz
(Frauen am Postdamer Platz), 1914
Woodcut. 20$^{1}/_{4}$ x 14$^{3}/_{4}$ in.
Sch. 221; Dube 239.
Lenders: Dr. and Mrs. Ernst Fischer, Albany

122
Three Boys (Prof. Fehr's Sons)
(Drei Knaben [Söhne Fehr]), 1915
Woodcut. $16^{11}/_{16}$ x 13 in.
Sch. 229; Dube 247.
Lenders: Dr. and Mrs. Ernst Fischer, Albany

123
Otto Müller, 1915
Color woodcut. $10^{7}/_{8}$ x $21^{9}/_{16}$ in.
Sch. 234; Dube 252.
Lender: Wolfgang Budczies, Bremen

124
Berlin City Railway (Stadtbahnbogen), 1915
Color lithograph. $19^7/_8$ x $23^1/_4$ in.
Sch. 306; Dube 292.
Lender: Grunwald Graphic Arts Foundation,
University of California, Los Angeles

125
**Conflicts; Peter Schlemihl Fighting
with his Shadow**
*(Kämpfe; Schlemihls Begegnung mit dem
Schatten),* from the illustrations to *Peter
Schlemihl* by Adelbert von Chamisso, 1915
Color woodcut. 12 x $11^5/_8$ in.
Sch. 270; Dube 268.
Lender: Museum of Fine Arts, Boston
(Bequest of W. G. Russell Allen)

126
Portrait of Henry van de Velde
(Dark version), 1917
Woodcut. $19^1/_2$ x $15^9/_{16}$ in.
Sch. 287; Dube 312.
Lenders: Dr. and Mrs. Ernst Fischer, Albany

127
Alpine Goatherd (Ziegenhirt), 1918
Woodcut. 18⁷/₈ x 15 in.
Sch. 365; Dube 334.
Lender: Museum of Fine Arts, Boston
(Bequest of W. G. Russell Allen)

128
Portrait of Ludwig Schames, 1918
Woodcut. 20⁷/₈ x 9⁷/₈ in.
Sch. 281; Dube 330.
Lenders: Dr. and Mrs. Ernst Fischer, Albany

129
The Meeting of Man and Woman
(Die Begegnung von Mann und Weib),
from the illustrations to *Triumph of Love*
by Petrarch, 1918
Woodcut. 14³/₈ x 12³/₁₆ in.
Sch. 316; Dube 343.
Lenders: Dr. and Mrs. Ernst Fischer, Albany

130

Attraction and Repulsion
(Anziehung und Abstossung), from the
illustrations to *Triumph of Love* by Petrarch,
1918
Woodcut. 14^{7}/$_{16}$ x 12^{7}/$_{16}$ in.
Sch. 317; Dube 344.
Lenders: Dr. and Mrs. Ernst Fischer, Albany

131

Man's Loss of Individuality
(Die Entselbstung des Mannes), from the
illustrations to *Triumph of Love* by Petrarch,
1918
Woodcut. 14^{3}/$_{16}$ x 9^{7}/$_{8}$ in.
Sch. 321; Dube 348.
Lenders: Dr. and Mrs. Ernst Fischer, Albany

132

Eternal Longing
(Die ewige Sehnsucht), from the illustrations
to *Triumph of Love* by Petrarch, 1918
Woodcut. 14^{9}/$_{16}$ x 12^{3}/$_{16}$ in.
Sch. 323; Dube 350.
Lenders: Dr. and Mrs. Ernst Fischer, Albany

154

133
The Gorge (Tobel), 1919
Color woodcut. 13³/₄ x 24³/₄ in.
Sch. 409; Dube 387.
Lender: Wolfgang Budczies, Bremen

134
Winter Moonlight (Wintermondnacht), 1919
Color woodcut. 12¹/₁₆ x 11⁵/₈ in.
Sch. 360; Dube 390.
Lender: The Museum of Modern Art,
New York (Abby Aldrich Rockefeller Fund)

135
The Sick One (Der Kranke), 1919
Woodcut. $5^{7}/_{8}$ x $4^{3}/_{8}$ in.
Sch. 346; Dube 401.
Lenders: Dr. and Mrs. Ernst Fischer, Albany

136
Woman in the Night (Frau in der Nacht), 1919
Woodcut. $22^{13}/_{16}$ x 13 in.
Sch. 389; Dube 405.
Lenders: Dr. and Mrs. Ernst Fischer, Albany

137
Haymakers (Heuer), 1920
Color woodcut. 12⁵/₁₆ x 24³/₈ in.
Sch. 401; Dube 421.
Lenders: Dr. and Mrs. Ernst Fischer, Albany

138
Portrait of the Dancer Nina Hard
(Kopf der Tänzerin Nina Hard), 1921
Drypoint in color. 12⁵/₁₆ x 9⁷/₈ in.
Sch. 387; Dube 385.
Lender: Fogg Art Museum, Harvard University
(Gift of Meta and Paul J. Sachs)

139
Melancholy Girl
(Melancholisches Mädchen), 1922
Color woodcut. 27¹/₂ x 15³/₄ in.
Sch. 465; Dube 480.
Lender: Museum of Fine Arts, Boston
(Bequest of W. G. Russell Allen)

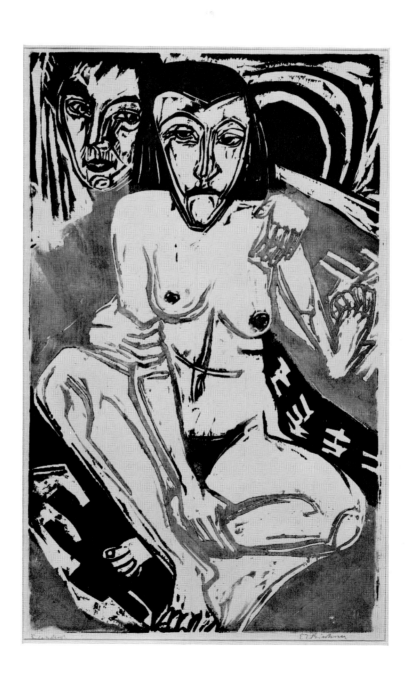

140
Modern Bohemia (Bohême moderne), 1924
Woodcut. 21$^{1}/_{4}$ x 33$^{1}/_{4}$ in.
Sch. 576; Dube 525.
Lender: The Museum of Modern Art,
New York (Curt Valentin Bequest)

141
Mountain Melancholy (Self-Portrait)
(Melancholie der Berge [Selbstbildnis]), 1929
Color woodcut. 19$^{11}/_{16}$ x 13$^{3}/_{4}$ in.
Not in Sch.; Dube 615.
Lender: Wolfgang Budczies, Bremen

142
Dr. Frederic Bauer, 1933
Color woodcut. 19³/₄ x 13³/₄ in.
Not in Sch.; Dube 633.
Lender: The Museum of Modern Art,
New York (Abby Aldrich Rockefeller Fund)

143
Color Dance (Farbentanz), 1933
Color woodcut. 19¹/₂ x 14 in.
Not in Sch.; Dube 636.
Lender: Anonymous loan

144
Three Nudes in the Forest
(Drei Akte im Walde), 1933
Color woodcut. 13⁷/₈ x 19⁵/₈ in.
Not in Sch.; Dube 637.
Lender: The Museum of Modern Art,
New York (Curt Valentin Bequest)

146
Illustrations for *Das Stiftsfräulein und der Tod* (The Pensioner and Death) by Alfred Döblin, Berlin, 1913
Woodcut illustrations and cover by Kirchner
Quarto
Collection: Mrs. Selma H. Sobin, Boston
Lender: Busch-Reisinger Museum, Harvard University (Gift of Mrs. Selma H. Sobin)

Reference: C. Kuhn, *German Expressionism, and Abstract Art; The Harvard Collections,* Supplement, 1967.

147
Nude (Akt), ca. 1910
Polychromed wood. 14³/₄ x 6⁷/₈ x 4³/₄ in.
Signed, under the base: *E. L. Kirchner*
Wilmersdorf Durlacherstr. 14 II
Lender: Galerie Wolfgang Ketterer, Munich

148
Nude (Stehender weiblicher Akt),
ca. 1919–20
Polychromed wood. Ht.: 24⁷/₈ in.
Signed, sole of right foot: *E L K*
Collection: Dr. Gervais
Lender: Galerie Springer, Berlin

Reference: W. Grohmann, *Das Werk Ernst*
Ludwig Kirchners, 1926, (pl. 55); Brücke
Museum, Berlin, *Brücke Museum; Verzeich-*
nis der zur Eröffnung ausgestellten Werke
September 1967 bis März 1968, 1967, no. 115
(pl. 30)

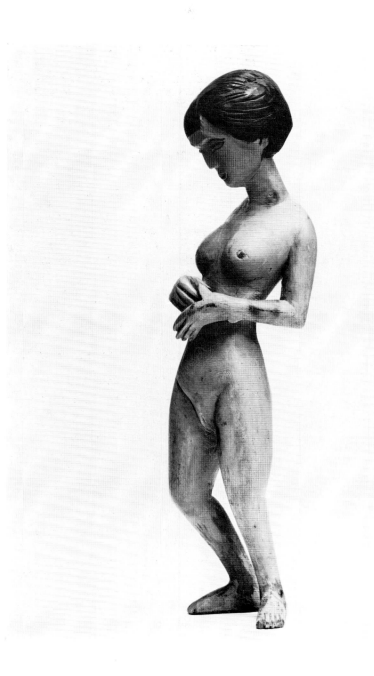

Selected Bibliography

More extensive bibliographies may be found in the catalogue of the Kirchner exhibition organized by the Kunstverein für die Rheinlande und Westfalen, presented at the Kunsthalle, Düsseldorf, 1960, and in the monograph and catalogue raisonné of Kirchner's oil paintings by Dr. Donald E. Gordon, 1968.

Published Writings of Ernst Ludwig Kirchner

Programm der Brücke, Dresden, 1906. Reprinted in H. Roethel, *Modern German Painting,* 1957.

Introduction to catalogue, *Die Brücke,* Galerie Arnold, Dresden, 1910.

Chronik der KG Brücke, Berlin, 1913. Reprinted in H. Roethel, *Modern German Painting,* 1957.

"Glaubensbekenntnisse eines Malers," *Die literarische Gesellschaft,* 1919, p. 24. Reprinted in *Das Kunstblatt,* no. 6, 1919, p. 168.

Catalogue text, *Kirchner,* Galerie Ludwig Schames, Frankfurt am Main, 1919. Reprinted in *Neues Winterthurer Tageblatt,* June 30, 1938.

Marsalle, L. de (pseudonym), "Zeichnungen von E. L. Kirchner," *Genius,* no. 2, 1920, pp. 216–34.

Marsalle, L. de, "Über Kirchners Graphik," *Genius,* no. 2, 1921, pp. 250–63. Reprinted in part in H. Wingler, *Die Brücke; Kunst im Aufbruch,* 1954.

"In Memoriam Ludwig Schames," *Der Querschnitt,* 1922, pp. 156–57.

"Zur Rundfrage 'Ein neuer Naturalismus,'" *Das Kunstblatt,* no. 9, 1922, pp. 375–76.

Marsalle, L. de, "Über die Schweizer Arbeiten von E. L. Kirchner," *Schweizer Arbeit von E. L. Kirchner,* Galerie Ludwig Schames, Frankfurt am Main, 1922. Reprinted in H. Wingler, *Wie sie einander sahen; moderne Maler im Urteil ihrer Gefährten,* 1957.

Text in P. Westheim, *Künstlerbekenntnisse,* Potsdam, 1925, p. 232.

Marsalle, L. de, "Über die plastischen Arbeiten E. L. Kirchners," *Der Cicerone,* no. 14, 1925, pp. 695–701.

"Die Kunst in Basel," *Das Kunstblatt,* no. 9, 1926, pp. 321–30.

"Die Kunst der Malerei; ein paar Worte zur Ausstellung meiner Bilder in Davos," *Davoser Zeitung,* no. 302, December 24, 1926.

"Kunstwerk und Kritik," *Davoser Zeitung,* no. 3, January 5, 1927.

"Albert Müller (Nachruf)," *Das Kunstblatt,* no. 5, 1927, p. 189.

Marsalle, L. de, introduction to catalogue, *Kirchner,* Galerie Aktuaryus, Zürich, 1927, pp. 5–12.

"Zum Gedächtnis Albert Müllers," in catalogue, *Gedächtnisausstellung A. Müller,* Kunsthalle, Basel, 1927, pp. 6–8.

"Hermann Scherer (Nachruf)," *Das Kunstblatt,* no. 9, 1927, p. 326.

Text in catalogue, *Gedächtnisausstellung H. Scherer,* Kunsthalle, Basel, 1928, pp. 3–4.

"Offener Brief an die Basler Vereinigung Rot-Blau," *Das Kunstblatt,* no. 5, 1929, p. 155.

"Bemerkungen über Leben und Arbeit," *Das Werk,* no. 1, 1930, pp. 2–4. Reprinted in W. Grohmann, *Bildende Kunst und Architektur,* 1953, pp. 365–66.

"Randglossen zum Artikel R. Arnheims: 'Klee für Kinder,'" *Das Kunstblatt,* no. 3, 1930, pp. 91–92. Response in R. Arnheim, "Brief an den Maler Kirchner," 1930 (see Articles on Kirchner).

"Zur Rundfrage 'Wovon man nicht spricht: die Wertsteigerung an Werken moderner Kunst',"* Das Kunstblatt,* no. 2, 1931, p. 39.

Marsalle, L. de, text in catalogue, *Kirchner,* Kunsthalle, Bern, 1933, pp. 14–16.

"Anfänge und Ziel," *Kroniek van hedendagsche Kunst en Kultur,* no. 1, 1935, p. 5–9.

"Ein paar Worte zur Arbeit," *Kroniek van hedendagsche Kunst en Kultur,* no. 10, 1937, p. 306.

"Ein paar Worte zu den Bildern," in catalogue, *Kirchner,* Kunsthalle, Basel, 1937, p. 20.

"Ernst Ludwig Kirchner über Kunst (4 nachgelassene Texte)," *Galerie und Sammler,* no. 4, 1939, p. 70.

"Die Arbeit E. L. Kirchners," manuscript. Published in part in catalogue, *Kirchner,* Gutekunst und Klipstein, Bern, 1954–55, pp. 7–12.

Published Letters of Ernst Ludwig Kirchner

to Frederic Bauer, January 26, 1928. In catalogue, *E. L. Kirchner – Brücke,* Galerie R. N. Ketterer, Campione, 1964.

to Eberhard Grisebach, Botho Gräf, and Helene Spengler. In L. Grisebach, ed., *Maler des Expressionismus,* 1962, pp. 40–41, 52–147.

to Niels von Holst, May 2, 1931. In catalogue, *Kirchner,* Frankfurter Kunstkabinett, 1954, p. 16.

to Ulrich Kirchner. In *Das Kunstwerk,* no. 3, 1951, pp. 14–21.

to Ulrich Kirchner. In catalogue, *Kirchner,* Frankfurter Kunstkabinett, 1954, pp. 17–20.

to Albert Müller. In *Werk,* XLII, no. 5, 1955, pp. 164–165.

to Curt Valentin, April 17, 1937. In catalogue, *Kirchner,* Curt Valentin Gallery, New York, 1952. Reprinted in C. Valentin, "A Letter from E. L. Kirchner," *The Minneapolis Institute of Arts Bulletin,* XLII, no. 8, 1953, pp. 37–38.

to Wilhelm R. Valentiner. In catalogue, *Kirchner,* North Carolina Museum of Art, Raleigh, 1958, pp. 39–48.

to Nele and Henry van de Velde. In E. Kirchner, *Briefe an Nele,* 1961, passim.

to Fritz Winter, May 3, 1929. In catalogue, *Sammlung Dr. F. Bauer, Davos,* Nuremberg, Munich, Freiburg, Mannheim, Berlin, 1952–53, pp. 9–10.

Monographs

Dube, Annemarie and Wolf-Dieter, *E. L. Kirchner; das graphische Werk,* 2 vols., München, Prestel-Verlag, 1967.

Göpel, Erhard, *Ernst Ludwig Kirchner; Farbige Graphik,* München, Piper, 1959.

Gordon, Donald E., *Ernst Ludwig Kirchner*, Cambridge, Harvard University Press, 1968.

Grisebach, Lothar, *E. L. Kirchners Davoser Tagebuch; Eine Darstellung des Malers und eine Sammlung seiner Schriften*, Köln, DuMont Schauberg, 1968.

Grohmann, Will, *Zeichnungen von Ernst Ludwig Kirchner*, Dresden, Arnold, 1925.

Grohmann, Will, *Das Werk Ernst Ludwig Kirchners*, München, Kurt Wolff, 1926.

Grohmann, Will, *E. L. Kirchner*, N. Y., Arts, 1961, translation of the German edition, Stuttgart, Kohlhammer, 1958.

Heynig, Annemarie, *E. L. Kirchner; Graphik*, München, Prestel-Verlag, 1961.

Schiefler, Gustav, *Die Graphik Ernst Ludwig Kirchners bis 1916*, Vol. I, Berlin-Charlottenburg, Euphorion-Verlag, 1927.

Schiefler, Gustav, *Die Graphik Ernst Ludwig Kirchners, 1917–1927*, Vol. II, Berlin-Charlottenburg, Euphorion-Verlag, 1931.

Wingler, Hans Maria, *E. L. Kirchner; 46 Holzschnitte*, Feldafing, Buchheim-Verlag, 1954.

General Works

Apollonio, Umbro, *"Die Brücke" e la cultura dell'espressionismo*, Venezia, Alfieri, 1952.

Bahr, Hermann, *Expressionismus*, München, Delphin Verlag, 1918.

Barr, Alfred H., Jr., *Painting and Sculpture in the Museum of Modern Art*, N. Y., The Museum of Modern Art, 1948, pp. 78, 79, 311.

Barr, Alfred H., Jr., *Masters of Modern Art*, N. Y., The Museum of Modern Art, 1954, p. 60.

Bolliger, Hans, "Die Publikationen und Dokumente der Künstlergruppe 'Brücke,'" *Philobiblon*, no. 1, 1959, pp. 41–71.

Buchheim, Lothar-Günther, *Deutsche Graphik des XX. Jahrhunderts*, Feldafing, Buchheim-Verlag, 1956, pp. 15, 62.

Buchheim, Lothar-Günther, *Die Künstlergemeinschaft Brücke*, Feldafing, Buchheim-Verlag, 1956.

Dressler, Adolf, *Deutsche Kunst und entartete Kunst*, München, Deutscher Volksverlag, 1938.

Fechter, Paul, *Der Expressionismus*, München, Piper, 1914.

Gerold, Karl Gustav, *Deutsche Malerei unserer Zeit*, München, Desch-Verlag, 1956.

Grisebach, Lothar, ed., *Maler des Expressionismus in Briefwechsel mit Eberhard Grisebach*, Hamburg, Christian Wegner Verlag, 1962.

Grohmann, Will, "Expressionismus," *Documents; Monthly Review of German Problems, German Contemporary Art* (special number), 1952.

Grohmann, Will, *Bildende Kunst und Architektur*, Berlin, Suhrkamp, 1953, pp. 52–55 ff. (Zwischen den beiden Kriegen, 3).

Grohmann, Will, *The Expressionists*, N. Y., Harry N. Abrams, 1957.

Grote, Ludwig, *Deutsche Kunst im zwanzigsten Jahrhundert*, München, Prestel-Verlag, 1953.

Grote, Ludwig, *Europäische Malerei in deutschen Galerien; Meister des 20. Jahrhunderts*, München, Prestel-Verlag, 1964.

Haendler, Gerhard, *German Painting in Our Time*, Berlin, Rembrandt-Verlag, 1956. Translation of the German edition, Berlin, Rembrandt-Verlag, 1956.

Haftmann, Werner, *Malerei im 20. Jahrhundert*, 2 vols., München, Prestel-Verlag, 1954–55 (rev. ed., 1962).

Hartlaub, G. F., *Die neue deutsche Graphik*, Berlin, Reiss, 1920.

Hartlaub, G. F., *Die Graphik des Expressionismus in Deutschland*, Stuttgart, Hatje, 1947, pp. 31–32, 58.

Hausenstein, Wilhelm, *Über Expressionismus in der Malerei*, Berlin, Reiss, 1919 (Tribüne der Kunst und Zeit, 2).

Hildebrandt, Hans, *Der Expressionismus in der Malerei*, Stuttgart, Reiss, 1919.

Hildebrandt, Hans, *Die Kunst des 19. und 20. Jahrhunderts*, 1st ed., Potsdam, Athenaion, 1924 (rev. ed., 1931).

Hofmann, Werner, *Expressionist Watercolors*, 1905–1920, N. Y., Harry N. Abrams, 1967. Translation of the German edition.

Holzinger, Ernst, "E. L. Kirchner," *Die grossen Deutschen*, Vol. V, Berlin, Propyläen-Verlag, 1957.

Justi, Ludwig, *Neue Kunst; Ein Führer zu den Gemälden der sogenannten Expressionisten in der National-Galerie*, Berlin, Julius Bard, 1921, pp. 30–31.

Kern, Walter, *Gedanken und Aufsätze über Kunst*, Zürich, Verlag Oprecht, 1940, pp. 35–41.

Kern, Walter, *Graubünden in der Malerei*, Zürich, Verlag Oprecht, 1941.

Kuhn, Charles L. and Rosenberg, Jakob, *German Expressionism and Abstract Art; The Harvard Collections*, Cambridge, Harvard University Press, 1957 (supplement, 1967).

Landau, Rom, *Der unbestechliche Minos*, Hamburg, Harder-Verlag, 1925, pp. 69–71.

Myers, Bernard, *The German Expressionists: a Generation in Revolt*, N. Y., Frederick A. Praeger, 1957, pp. 125–38. Translation of the German edition, Köln, DuMont, 1957.

Nemitz, Fritz, *Deutsche Malerei in der Gegenwart*, München, Piper, 1948.

Nolde, Emil, *Jahre der Kämpfe*, Berlin, Julius Bard, 1934.

Platte, Hans, *Die Kunst des 20. Jahrhunderts*, München, 1957.

Platte, Hans, *Gustav Schiefler; Aus den Erinnerungen von Luise Schiefler*, Hamburg, Hans Christians Verlag, 1965.

Pommeranz-Liedtke, Gerhard, *Der graphische Zyklus von Max Klinger bis zur Gegenwart; Ein Beitrag zur Entwicklung der deutschen Graphik von 1880 bis 1955*, Berlin, Deutsche Akademie der Künste, 1956.

Powys, Llewelyn, *Swiss Essays*, London, John Lane, 1947, pp. 19–26.

Rave, Paul Ortwin, *Kunstdiktatur im dritten Reich*, Hamburg, Gebr. Mann, 1949.

Raynal, Maurice *et al, Geschichte der modernen Malerei; Fauvismus und Expressionismus,* Vol. II, Geneva, Albert Skira, 1950, pp. 80–83, 114–15, 137–38, 151.

Read, Herbert, *Art Now: An Introduction to the Theory of Modern Painting and Sculpture,* London, Faber and Faber, 1933, pp. 87–88.

Röthel, Hans Konrad, *Modern German Painting,* N. Y., Reynal, 1957. Translation of the German edition, Wiesbaden, Emil Vollmer, 1957.

Roh, Franz, *"Entartete" Kunst; Kunstbarbarei im dritten Reich,* Hannover, Fackelträger, 1962.

Sachs, Paul J., *Modern Prints and Drawings: A Guide to a Better Understanding of Modern Draughtsmanship,* N. Y., Alfred A. Knopf, 1954, pp. 126–27.

Sauerland, Max, *Die Kunst der letzten dreissig Jahre,* Berlin, Rembrandt-Verlag, 1935 (2d ed., 1948).

Scheffler, Karl, *Geschichte der europäischen Malerei vom Impressionismus bis zur Gegenwart,* Berlin, Cassirer, 1927.

Schmidt, Georg, *Malerei in Deutschland 1900 bis 1918: 1918–1955.* 2 vols., Königstein im Taunus, Karl Robert Langewiesche Nachfolger, Hans Köster, 1959–60 (2d ed., 1960).

Schmidt, Paul Ferdinand, *Geschichte der modernen Malerei,* Stuttgart, Kohlhammer, 1952, pp. 171–76.

Selz, Peter, *German Expressionist Painting,* Berkeley, University of California Press, 1957.

Thoene, Peter, *Modern German Art,* Harmondsworth, Penguin Books, 1938, pp. 48–50.

Westheim, Paul, *Das Holzschnittbuch,* Potsdam, 1921.

Westheim, Paul, *Für und Wider,* Potsdam, Kiepenheuer, 1923.

Wingler, Hans Maria, *Die Brücke; Kunst im Aufbruch,* Feldafing, Buchheim-Verlag, 1954.

Wingler, Hans Maria, *Wie sie einander sahen; Moderne Maler im Urteil ihrer Gefährten,* München, Langen and Müller, 1957, pp. 46–47.

Zigrosser, Carl, *The Expressionists: A Survey of their Graphic Art,* N. Y., Braziller, 1957, pp. 11–15.

Articles on Kirchner

Arnheim, Rudolf, "Brief an den Maler Kirchner." *Die Weltbühne,* no. 11, 1930, pp. 394–98. (Response to Kirchner's "Randglossen zum Artikel R. Arnheims: Klee für Kinder," *Das Kunstblatt,* no. 3, 1930, pp. 91–92).

Branger, Erhard. "Zu Kirchners Bergbildern," *Davoser Revue,* no. 9, 1938, pp. 189–92.

Ettlinger, L. D., "German Expressionism and Abstract Art," *The Burlington Magazine,* CX, no. 781, 1968, pp. 191–201.

"Exhibition of more than Thirty Drawings, Woodcuts and Etchings at New Art Center," *Arts,* XXXI, January, 1957, p. 59.

Gläser, Kurt, "E. L. Kirchner bei Cassirer," *Kunst und Künstler,* no. 1, 1924, pp. 62-63.

Gordon, Donald E., "Kirchner in Dresden," *Art Bulletin,* XLVIII, nos. 3–4, 1966, pp. 335–66.

Gräef, Botho, "E. L. Kirchner," *Das Kunstblatt,* no. 3 (Sonderheft Kirchner), 1923, pp. 65–77.

Grohmann, Will, "Über die Graphik von E. L. Kirchner," *Das Kunstblatt,* no. 3 (Sonderheft Kirchner-Graphik), 1925, pp. 65–79.

Grohmann, Will, "E. L. Kirchner," *Davoser Blätter,* no. 36, 1926, pp. 1–2.

Grohmann, Will, "Die Schweizer Jahre E. L. Kirchners; Umkehr und Einkehr," *Werk,* XLII, no. 6, 1955, pp. 157–63.

Henze, Anton, "E. L. Kirchner und Carl Hagemann; Zur Geschichte der Sammlung Hagemann und der Tragödie von Essen," *Das Kunstwerk,* no. 4, 1955–56, pp. 9–19.

Heynig, Annemarie, "Natur und Landschaft im Werk E. L. Kirchners," *Christliche Kunstblätter,* no. 4, 1958, pp. 11–16.

Jedlicka, Gotthard, "E. L. Kirchner," *Galerie und Sammler,* no. 4, 1939, pp. 63–71.

Kern, Walter, "E. L. Kirchner, seine Bilder von 1907 bis 1929," *Das Kunstblatt,* no. 6, 1930, pp. 160–65.

Kern, Walter, "Kirchners *Tod,"* *Neue Schweizer Rundschau,* no. 4, 1938, pp. 252–55.

Kessler, Charles, "Sun Worship and Anxiety; Nature, Nakedness, and Nihilism in German Expressionist Painting," *Magazine of Art,* XLV, no. 7, 1952, pp. 304–312.

Kirchner, E. L., *Davoser Blätter,* no. 17, 1921, pp. 1–3.

Kirchner, Hans Walter, "E. L. Kirchner: aus Schriften und Briefen; Aus nachgelassenen Briefen," *Das Kunstwerk,* no. 3, 1951, pp. 14–21.

"Kirchner, Early Pioneer of Modern German Painting, Exhibition Buchholz Gallery," *Art News,* no. 36, 1937, p. 13.

"Kirchner Exhibition at New Art Center," *Art News,* LVII, no. 3, 1959, p. 11.

Kornfeld, Eberhard and Bolliger, Hans, "Ernst Ludwig Kirchners Schweizer Jahre," *Du,* August, 1964, pp. 2–17.

Kuhn, Charles L., "Ernst Ludwig Kirchner, Expressionist Bridge; Exhibition at Busch-Reisinger Museum," *Art News,* XLIX, no. 9, 1951, pp. 36–38.

Myers, Bernard, "Postwar Art in Germany," *College Art Journal,* no. 3, 1951, pp. 251–56.

Myers, Bernard, "E. L. Kirchner and 'Die Brücke'," *Magazine of Art,* XLV, no. 1, 1952, pp. 20–26.

Poeschel, Erwin, "Ausstellung E. L. Kirchner im Schulhaus Davos-Platz," *Davoser Revue,* no. 305, 1926.

Poort, Herman, "E. L. Kirchner," *Das Kunstblatt,* no. 9, 1926, pp. 331–50.

Porter, Fairfield, "Kirchner Exhibition, Valentin Gallery," *Art News,* LI, May, 1952, p. 42.

Redslob, Edwin, "E. L. Kirchners Elisabethenufer," *Genius,* I, no. 1, 1919, p. 57.

Rosenberg, Jakob, "German Expressionist Printmakers," *Magazine of Art,* XXXVIII, no. 8, 1945, pp. 300–05.

Rosner, Charles, "Memorial Exhibition, Davos Art Society," *London Studio,* XVI, 1938, p. 270.

Sauerland, Max, "Holzbildwerke von Kirchner, Heckel und Schmidt-Rottluff," *Museum der Gegenwart,* no. 3, 1930, pp. 101–11.

Schapire, Rosa, "E. L. Kirchner," *Der Kreis,* no. 3, 1927, pp. 143–47.

Schenk zu Schweinsberg, Eberhard Freiherr, "Die Sammlung Hagemann in Frankfurt am Main," *Museum der Gegenwart,* Berlin, 1931, pp. 99–110.

Schiefler, Gustav, "E. L. Kirchner in Davos," *Das Kunstblatt,* no. 3 (Sonderheft Kirchner), 1923, pp. 81–91.

Schiefler, Gustav, "E. L. Kirchner als Graphiker," *Neue Zürcher Zeitung,* June 15, 1927.

Schiefler, Gustav, "E. L. Kirchners Entwürfe für Wandgestaltung in einem Festsaal des Folkwang-Museums in Essen," *Das Kunstblatt,* no. 2, 1929, pp. 33–45.

Schmalenbach, Werner, "E. L. Kirchner," *Werk,* no. 1, 1948, pp. 18–23.

Schmidt, Georg, "Die Holzschnitte von E. L. Kirchner zu Georg Heym 'Umbra vitae'," *Das Werk,* no. 8, 1925, pp. 241–44.

Schmidt, Georg, "Rot-Blau; Ein Kapitel Basler Kunst," *Das Werk,* no. 2, 1927, pp. 38–44, 51–56.

Selz, Peter, "E. L. Kirchners 'Chronik der Brücke'," *College Art Journal,* X, no. 1, 1950, pp. 50–54.

Thieme-Becker, *Allgemeines Lexikon der bildenden Künstler,* Leipzig, Seemann, 1927, XX, pp. 360–62. ("E. L. Kirchner," by Rosa Schapire.)

Tyler, Parker, "Emil Nolde and E. L. Kirchner at Museum of Modern Art," *Art News,* LIV, no. 12, 1955, p. 51.

Valentin, Curt, "A Letter from E. L. Kirchner," *The Minneapolis Institute of Arts Bulletin,* XLII, no. 8, 1953, pp. 37–38.

Valentiner, Wilhelm R., "Expressionism in Abstract Painting," *The Art Quarterly,* IV, no. 3, 1941, pp. 210–39.

Van de Velde, Nele, "Ein Tag bei Kirchner auf der Staffelalp," *Genius,* II, no. 2, 1920, pp. 282–92.

Vollmer, Hans, "E. L. Kirchner," *Allgemeines Lexikon der bildenden Künstler des XX. Jahrhunderts.* Leipzig, Seemann, 1956, III, pp. 49–50.

Westheim, Paul, "L'impressionisme et l'expressionisme en Allemagne," *L'Amour de l'art,* no. 15, 1934, p. 429.

Westheim, Paul, "E. L. Kirchner," *Kroniek van kunst en kultur,* Amsterdam, 1955, pp. 231–33.

Wiese, Erich, "Zeichnungen von E. L. Kirchner," *Monatshefte für Bücherfreunde und Graphik-sammler,* no. 2, 1925, pp. 459–68.

Zoege von Manteuffel, Claus, "Kirchner-Nachlass in Basel," *Das Kunstwerk,* no. 6, 1951, pp. 59–60.

"Zur Ausstellung von Werken E. L. Kirchners," *Davoser Revue,* no. 3, 1926, pp. 10–14.

Selected Exhibition Catalogues

1913

Folkwang-Museum, Hagen, *E. L. Kirchner: Gemälde und Graphik,* Oct. 1913.

Kunstsalon Fritz Gurlitt, Berlin, *E. L. Kirchner,* Nov. 1913.

1914

Kunstverein, Jena, *E. L. Kirchner,* Feb.–Mar. 1914.

1916

Galerie Ludwig Schames, Frankfurt am Main, *E. L. Kirchner,* Feb.–Mar. 1916.

1917

Kunstverein, Jena, *E. L. Kirchner,* Mar. 1917.

Buchhandlung Erfurt, Davos, *E. L. Kirchner: Holz-schnitte,* Oct.–Nov. 1917.

1918

Kunsthaus, Zürich, *E. L. Kirchner,* Mar. 10–Apr. 2, 1918.

Galerie Ludwig Schames, Frankfurt am Main, *E. L. Kirchner,* 1918.

1919

Galerie Ludwig Schames, Frankfurt am Main, *E. L. Kirchner,* Feb.–Mar. 1919. Includes "Einige Worte über die Arbeit von E. L. Kirchner" by Botho Gräef, p. 2.

1920

Galerie Ludwig Schames, Frankfurt am Main, *E. L. Kirchner: Graphik,* Jan.–Feb. 1920. Includes: "Ernst Ludwig Kirchner, 5 Gedichte" by Carl Theodor Bluth, pp. 11–20, and "Über das graphische Werk von E. L. Kirchner" by Eberhard Grisebach.

Kunsthalle, Bremen, *Munch und die Künstler der "Brücke,"* 1920.

1921

Kronprinzenpalais, Berlin, *E. L. Kirchner,* Feb. 1921.

Galerie Ludwig Schames, Frankfurt am Main, *E. L. Kirchner,* Apr. 1921.

1922

Galerie Ludwig Schames, Frankfurt am Main, *Schweizer Arbeit von E. L. Kirchner,* 1922.

Kunstverein, Erfurt, *E. L. Kirchner,* 1922.

1923

Kunsthalle, Basel, *E. L. Kirchner,* June 3–24, 1923.

Paul Cassirer Galerie, Berlin, *E. L. Kirchner,* Nov.–Dec. 1923.

Galerie Commeter, Hamburg, *E. L. Kirchner: Graphik,* Jan. 1923.

Galerie Ludwig Schames, Frankfurt am Main, *E. L. Kirchner: Graphik,* May 1923.

Goldschmidt und Wallerstein, Berlin, *E. L. Kirchner, Zeichnungen und Aquarelle,* Oct. 1923.

1924

Kunstverein, Winterthur, *E. L. Kirchner,* June 22–July 13, 1924.

Paul Cassirer Galerie, Berlin, *E. L. Kirchner: Graphik,* Oct.–Nov. 1924.

1925

Galerie Arnold, Dresden, *E. L. Kirchner,* Apr. 1925.

Galerie Ludwig Schames, Frankfurt am Main, *E. L. Kirchner,* Nov.–Dec. 1925.

Galerie Commeter, Hamburg, *E. L. Kirchner: Graphik,* Oct.–Nov. 1925.

1926

Paul Cassirer Galerie, Berlin, *E. L. Kirchner,* Nov. 1926.

Kunstsalon Fides, Dresden, *E. L. Kirchner,* Nov.– Dec. 1926.

Kunstgesellschaft, Schulhaus Davos-Platz, Davos, *E. L. Kirchner,* Dec. 27, 1926–Jan. 1927.

Graphisches Kabinett, Munich, *E. L. Kirchner: Graphik,* 1926.

1927

Kunstverein, Wiesbaden and Kunstsalon Fides, Dresden, *E. L. Kirchner, May–June* 1927.

Galerie Aktuaryus, Zürich, *E. L. Kirchner: Aquarelle und Zeichnungen,* June–July 1927.

1928

Kunstverein, Hannover, *Deutscher Künstlerbund,* Feb. 19–Apr. 15, 1928.

1931

J. B. Neumann and Günther Franke, Munich, *E. L. Kirchner,* 1931.

The Museum of Modern Art, New York, *German Painting and Sculpture,* Mar. 13–Apr. 26, 1931. Includes "German Painting and Sculpture" by Alfred H. Barr, Jr.

1933

Kunsthalle, Bern, *E. L. Kirchner,* Mar. 5–Apr. 17, 1933. Foreword by Max Huggler, pp. 9–13.

1934

Galerie Commeter, Hamburg, *E. L. Kirchner: Holz- schnitte,* May 1934.

1935

Kupferstichkabinett, Basel. *E. L. Kirchner: Aquarelle und Zeichnungen,* May 13–June 23, 1935.

1937

Detroit Institute of Arts, *E. L. Kirchner,* Jan. 1937.

Buchholz Gallery–Curt Valentin, New York, *E. L. Kirchner,* Sept. 29–Oct. 27, 1937.

Kunsthalle, Basel, *E. L. Kirchner,* Oct. 30–Nov. 27, 1937.

Haus der Kunst, Munich, *Entartete Kunst,* summer, 1937.

1938

Kunstgesellschaft, Schulhaus Davos-Platz, Davos, *Graubünden in der Malerei und Gedächtnisaus- stellung E. L. Kirchner,* July 16–Aug. 7, 1938.

1939

Galerie Aktuaryus, Zürich, *Gedächtnis-Ausstellung Ernst Ludwig Kirchner,* Apr. 30–May 23, 1939.

Museum of Fine Arts, Springfield, Mass., *Modern German Art,* Jan. 10–30, 1939.

The Museum of Modern Art, New York, *Art in Our Time,* summer, 1939.

Institute of Modern Art, Boston, *Contemporary German Art,* Nov. 2–Dec. 9, 1939.

1943

Kunststube im Rösslyn, Zürich, *E. L. Kirchner und sein Kreis,* 1943. Foreword by Walter Kern.

1945

Baltimore Museum of Art, *German Expressionism* (Booth Collection), 1945.

1947

Galerie Bremer, Berlin, *E. L. Kirchner,* Jan. 12–end of Feb. 1947. Foreword by Carl Linfert.

Galerie d'Art Moderne, Basel, *E. L. Kirchner,* Oct.– Nov. 1947. Foreword by Werner Schmalenbach.

1948

Galerie Bremer, Berlin, *E. L. Kirchner,* June 15– July 31, 1948. Foreword by Edwin Redslob.

Württembergischer Kunstverein, Stuttgart, *E. L. Kirchner: Aquarelle, Zeichnungen, Graphik,* May 29–July 4, 1948. Foreword by Erwin Petermann.

Kunsthalle, Bern, *Paula Modersohn und die Maler der "Brücke,"* July 3–Aug. 15, 1948. Includes "Die Künstlergruppe Brücke 1905 bis 1913" by W. F. Arntz.

1949

Galerie Günther Franke, Munich, *E. L. Kirchner,* 1949.

Stedelijk Museum, Amsterdam, *Expressionisme, van Gogh tot Picasso,* 1949.

1950

Kunstmuseum, St. Gallen, *E. L. Kirchner,* Oct. 15– Nov. 19, 1950.

Kunstverein, Hamburg, *E. L. Kirchner: Werke aus dem Nachlass, zum ersten Male in Deutschland, aus Anlass seines 70. Geburtstages,* Sept. 1950. Fore- word by Alfred Hentzen. Also shown at Kestner- gesellschaft, Hannover; Kunsthalle, Bremen; and Museum, Wuppertal-Elberfeld, Oct. 1950–Jan. 1951.

Busch-Reisinger Museum, Cambridge, Mass., *E. L. Kirchner,* Dec. 8, 1950–Jan. 12, 1951.

Städelsches Kunstinstitut, Frankfurt am Main, *Graphik von E. L. Kirchner,* 1950.

1951

Orangerie der Universität, Erlangen, *Kirchner und Nolde,* Nov. 4–20, 1951.

Galerie Jürg Stuker, Bern, *Bibliothek Ernst Ludwig Kirchner* (the artist's personal library), Feb. 19– Mar. 3, 1951.

University of Minnesota, Minneapolis, *German Expressionism,* Oct.–Nov. 1951.

1952

Kunsthaus, Zürich, *E. L. Kirchner,* Mar.–May 1952. Includes: "E. L. Kirchner" by Werner Schmalenbach, pp. 3–6; foreword by René Wehrli, pp. 8–9; "Lebens- daten und Bibliographie" by Hans Bolliger, pp. 10– 14.

Curt Valentin Gallery, New York, *E. L. Kirchner,* Apr.–May 1952.

Nuremberg, Munich, Freiburg, Mannheim, Berlin, *Sammlung Dr. F. Bauer, Davos,* 1952–53. Foreword by Ludwig Grote.

XXVI Biennale, Venice, *Brücke*, summer–autumn, 1952. Includes: "Le caratteristiche e lo stile del 'Brücke'" by H. K. Roethel, pp. 13–16; "Un contributo allo studio dell'espressionismo tedesco" by Walter Kern, pp. 24–28; "Die Brücke" by Eberhard Hanfstaengl, pp. 284–86.

1953

Stuttgarter Kunstkabinett, Stuttgart, *E. L. Kirchner*, Mar.–Apr. 1953.

Kunsthaus, Chur, *E. L. Kirchner: Gemälde und Graphik aus der Davoser Zeit*, July 19–Sept. 19, 1953.

Galerie Günther Franke, Munich, *E. L. Kirchner: Graphik*, May–June 1953.

Moderne Galerie Otto Stangl, Munich, *E. L. Kirchner: Weberei, Graphik und Plastik*, Nov.–Dec. 1953. Includes "Die Wollwebereien von Lise Gujer nach Entwürfen von E. L. Kirchner" by Hans Bolliger.

Kestner-Museum, Hannover, *Brücke-Mappen und Chronik*, July–Sept. 1953.

1954

Galerie Wilhelm Grosshennig, Düsseldorf, *E. L. Kirchner*, Oct.–Nov. 1954.

Gutekunst und Klipstein, Bern, *E. L. Kirchner*, Dec. 1954–Jan. 1955. Includes "Lebensdaten" by Eberhard W. Kornfeld.

Galerie Günther Franke, Munich, *E. L. Kirchner: Unbekanntes aus dem Schweizer Nachlass. Graphik*, Jan.–Feb. 1954.

Galerie Bremer, Berlin, *E. L. Kirchner: Graphik*, May 1954.

Kunsthalle, Bremen, *E. L. Kirchner: Graphik*, May–June 1954.

Frankfurter Kunstkabinett, Frankfurt am Main, *E. L. Kirchner: Graphik*, Oct.–Nov. 1954.

Munich, Cologne, Stuttgart, *E. L. Kirchner: Graphik*, 1954.

Museo civico, Turin, *Espressionismo e arte tedesca del 20° secolo*, summer, 1954.

Allan Frumkin Gallery, Chicago, *20th Century German Graphic Art*, 1954.

1955

Kestner-Museum, Hannover, *E. L. Kirchner: Graphik*, Jan.–Feb. 1955.

The Museum of Modern Art, New York, *E. L. Kirchner: Graphic Art*, Nov.–Dec. 1955.

Curt Valentin Gallery, New York, *Closing Exhibition*, June 1955.

Museum Fridericianum, Kassel, *Documenta; Kunst des 20. Jahrhunderts*, July–Sept. 1955.

Los Angeles County Museum, *German Expressionist Prints*, 1955.

1956

Württembergischer Kunstverein, Stuttgart, *E. L. Kirchner*, Sept.–Oct. 1956. Includes foreword by Ewald Rathke, pp. 3–4.

Galerie Meta Nierendorf, Berlin, *E. L. Kirchner: Aquarelle, Graphik, Zeichnungen*, Sept.–Nov. 1956.

New Art Center, New York, *E. L. Kirchner: Drawings and Graphic Art*, Dec. 1956–Jan. 1957.

Walker Art Center, Minneapolis, *Expressionism 1900–1955*, also shown at the Institute of Contemporary Art, Boston, San Francisco Museum of Art, Cincinnati Museum, Baltimore Museum of Art, and Albright Art Gallery, Buffalo, 1956–57.

Tate Gallery, London, *A Hundred Years of German Painting, 1850–1950*, 1956.

Klipstein und Kornfeld, Bern, *Von der Brücke zum Bauhaus. Aquarelle, Zeichnungen, Graphik*, Jan. 21–Feb. 18, 1956. Includes "Chronologie der Künstlergruppe 'Brücke'" by Hans Bolliger, pp. 6–7.

Borgenicht and Weyhe Galleries, New York, *German Watercolors, Drawings and Prints* (circulated to several American cities by the American Federation of Arts), 1956.

1957

Städtisches Museum, Lindau, *E. L. Kirchner*, Mar.–Apr. 1957.

Paul Kantor Gallery, Los Angeles, *E. L. Kirchner*, Apr. 8–May 3, 1957. Includes introduction by Gerald Nordland.

Fine Arts Associates, New York, *E. L. Kirchner*, Nov. 12–Dec. 7, 1957.

Schloss Gottorf, Schleswig, *Graphik der Brücke*, Apr.–May 1957. Includes text by Martin Urban, pp. 1–11.

World House Galleries, New York, *Expressionism; The Richard Feigen Collection*, Sept. 18–Dec. 7, 1957.

Albertina, Vienna, *Der Expressionismus*, autumn, 1957.

The Museum of Modern Art, New York, *German Art of the Twentieth Century*, Oct. 1–Dec. 8, 1957, also shown at the City Art Museum of St. Louis, through Feb. 24, 1958. Includes "Painting" by Werner Haftmann, pp. 13–140, and "Prints" by William S. Lieberman, pp. 185–217.

Quadriennale nazionale d'arte di Roma, Rome, *Arte tedesca al 1905 ad oggi*, also shown at the Palazzo della Permanento, Milan, 1957–58. Includes "Introduzione alla mostra d'arte tedesca" by Will Grohmann.

Pomona College, Claremont. *German Expressionist Painting, 1900–1950*, also shown at the University of California, Berkeley, and the Santa Barbara Museum. Oct. 1957–Feb. 1958.

1958

North Carolina Museum of Art, Raleigh, *E. L. Kirchner*, Jan.–Feb. 1958. Includes text by Wilhelm R. Valentiner, pp. 7–38.

Museum Folkwang, Essen, *Brücke 1905–1913, eine Künstlergemeinschaft*, Oct.–Dec. 1958. Includes "Einführung" and "Zeittafel der Künstlergruppe 'Brücke'" by Martin Urban, pp. 3–18.

Klipstein und Kornfeld, Bern, *Ausstellung Brücke, Jahresmappen 1906–1912. Graphik*, Oct. 1958. Catalogue by Hans Bolliger and E. W. Kornfeld. Includes "Zeittafel der Künstlergruppe 'Brücke'" by Martin Urban.

Galerie Günther Franke, Munich, *Bildnisse der ersten Hälfte des 20. Jahrhunderts*, 1958.

1959

New Art Center, New York, *E. L. Kirchner, Drawings and Graphic Art,* Mar. 2–14, 1959.

Städtische Galerie, Munich, *Die Maler der Brücke; Sammlung Buchheim,* June–July 1959.

Museum, Ulm, *Brücke,* 1959.

Boston, Milwaukee, Columbus, Minneapolis, *Expressionism,* Jan.–May 1959.

Marlborough Fine Art Ltd., London, *Art in Revolt, Germany 1905–1925,* Nov. 1959.

Berlin-Charlottenburg, Orangerie, *Triumph der Farbe,* 1959.

1960

Kunsthaus, Chur, *E. L. Kirchner,* July–Sept. 1960.

Kunsthalle, Düsseldorf, *E. L. Kirchner,* Sept.–Oct. 1960. Includes texts by Karlheinz Gabler, Annemarie Dube-Heynig, and Hans Bolliger.

Kunsthalle, Bremen, *Meisterwerke des deutschen Expressionismus,* also shown at Kunstverein, Hannover, Gemeentemuseum, The Hague, and Wallraf-Richartz-Museum, Cologne, Mar.–Nov. 1960, and Kunsthaus, Zürich, May–June 1961.

St. Louis University, *Paintings from the Collection of Mr. and Mrs. Morton D. May,* Feb.–July 1960, also shown in Denver, Los Angeles (UCLA), San Diego, San Francisco (De Young), Chicago, Youngstown, Akron, Pittsburgh, Washington, D. C. (Corcoran), and Baltimore, 1960–62, under the title *German Expressionist Paintings from the Collection of Mr. and Mrs. Morton D. May.*

1961

Galerie Meta Nierendorf, Berlin, *E. L. Kirchner: Zeichnungen,* Nov. 1961–Feb. 1962. Includes text by Florian Karsch.

Columbus, Ohio, Gallery of Fine Arts, *German Expressionism,* Feb. 10–Mar. 9, 1961.

Isaac Delgado Museum, New Orleans, *Expressionism,* Oct.–Dec. 1961.

Pasadena Art Museum, *German Expressionism,* 1961.

1962

Landesmuseum, Schleswig, *Die Maler der "Brücke,"* May 6–Aug. 12, 1962. Also shown at the Overbeck-Gesellschaft, Lübeck.

Haus der Kunst, Munich, *Entartete Kunst; Bildersturm vor 25 Jahren,* Oct. 25–Dec. 16, 1962.

Salonika, Athens, Beirut, *Deutsche Kunst von 1910 bis zur Gegenwart,* 1962–63.

1963

Galerie Nierendorf, Berlin, *E. L. Kirchner: Graphik,* June–Oct. 1963. Includes "E. L. Kirchner zum fünfundzwanzigsten Todestag" by Will Grohmann.

Galerie Welz, Salzburg, *E. L. Kirchner, Aquarelle und Graphik, Leihgaben aus Galerie Nierendorf,* July 29–Sept. 15, 1963.

The Jansen Art Studio, New York, *E. L. Kirchner: Watercolors and Drawings,* Oct. 28–Nov. 23, 1963.

Marlborough-Gerson Gallery, New York, *A Tribute to Curt Valentin,* Nov.–Dec. 1963.

J. L. Hudson Gallery, Detroit, *The W. R. Valentiner Memorial Exhibition,* Nov. 18, 1963–Jan. 2, 1964.

1964

Galleria d'Arte Contemporanea, Turin, *E. L. Kirchner,* Mar. 5–25, 1964.

Galerie R. N. Ketterer, Campione, *E. L. Kirchner,* summer, 1964. Includes "Ansprache zur Eröffnung der Ausstellung E. L. Kirchner, Stuttgart 1957" by Dr. F. Bauer.

Galerie R. N. Ketterer, Campione, *E. L. Kirchner – Brücke,* autumn, 1964. Includes "Brief an Dr. F. Bauer, 26. Januar, 1928" by E. L. Kirchner.

Galleria del Levante, Milan, *E. L. Kirchner: Drawings,* Jan. 8–Feb. 8, 1964.

Graphik-Kabinett G. D. Baedecker, Essen, *E. L. Kirchner: Zeichnungen,* Jan. 27–Feb. 29, 1964.

Tate Gallery, London, *Painters of the "Brücke,"* Oct.–Dec. 1964.

Museum Die Fähre, Saulgau/Württemberg, *Von Corinth bis Antes,* Sept. 20–Oct. 18, 1964.

Baltimore Museum of Art, *1914,* Oct. 6–Nov. 15, 1964.

Museum Fridericianum, Kassel, *Documenta III,* 1964.

1965

Spendhaus, Reutlingen, *E. L. Kirchner,* Oct.–Nov. 1965.

1966

Musée National d'Art Moderne, Paris, *Le fauvisme français et les debuts de l'expressionisme allemand,* 1966, also shown at the Haus der Kunst, Munich.

Amherst College, Mass., *German Art after World War I,* 1966.

1967

Kunsthalle, Basel, *E. L. Kirchner und Rot-Blau,* Sept.–Oct. 1967.

1968

Leonard Hutton Galleries, New York, *Fauves and Expressionists,* Apr.–June 1968.

Marlborough-Gerson Gallery, New York, *International Expressionism, Part I,* summer 1968.